ARE YOU MY DOG?

How to Find Your Best Friend

DR. JANET RUCKERT

TEN SPEED PRESS
BERKELEY, CALIFORNIA

DEDICATION

THIS BOOK is dedicated to the dogs who offer us their love, their playfulness, their service, and their friendship for life and to their owners who took the time and care to choose the right one.

I offer my appreciation to the dedicated members of the animal organizations who train and place dogs with the appropriate persons—the humane societies, dog orphan groups, Canine Companions for Independence, and trainers of seeing eye dogs and hearing ear dogs. I would like to acknowledge the breeders who work to produce happy, healthy puppies and the obedience trainers and clubs who help owners to educate and enjoy their dogs.

I thank my agent, Mel Burger, who may yet get a dog, Irene Webb who found the right family dog, Robert Windeler, and Janna Wong Healy. Special thanks to my talented editor, Patti Breitman, and to the staff of Ten Speed Press.

Finally, thanks to my Rottweilers, Lorelei and Delilah, who taught me patience, took me for walks when I needed time off, and offered encouragement when I needed a warm paw.

Jan Ruckert
Los Angeles, California
November 1989

1❦

TEN SPEED PRESS
Box 7123
Berkeley, Ca 94707

Cover design by Fifth Street Design
Illustrations by Jan Salerno
Text design by Paula Schlosser
Type set by Wilsted & Taylor

LIBRARY OF CONGRESS CATALOGING-IN-PUBLICATION DATA
Ruckert, Janet, 1926–
  Are you my dog? / by Janet Ruckert.
    p. cm.
  ISBN 0-89815-325-5 :
  1. Dogs. 2. Dogs—Selection. 3. Dog breeds. I. Title.
SF426.R84 1989
636.7'081—dc20   89-33573
                                                                CIP

Printed in the United States of America

1 2 3 4 5—93 92 91 90 89

Contents

Foreword

As a veterinarian, I am a firm believer in the old adage that an ounce of prevention is worth a pound of cure. So often I see behavior and relationship problems between dogs and their human families and companions that could be prevented. This book will go a long way in solving such problems for future first-time dog owners and for those people who have had dogs before and are looking to get a new one—and who want to find the best dog for their situation and particular needs.

Too often dog owners find themselves in situations where they wish they had been forewarned or had the benefit of hindsight. The "good medicine" of this book provides a wealth of wisdom to help ensure that dog owners have no regrets as to their choice of a dog or puppy; and have the promise of a satisfying relationship with the canine companion of their choice for many years to come.

Many would-be dog owners have special needs and requirements because they are in some way handicapped and have heard that a dog in one's life can make a world of difference. This special interest group will find this book of particular value in helping them realize the many benefits of having a well-trained and emotionally attuned dog at their side.

The dog was the first of all God's creatures to be domesticated, some 12–14,000 years ago, during the time that some historians and mythologists call the Golden Age. We owe our oldest animal companion much for its devotion and loyalty through the ages. Even though, after all these years, we may regard dogs as our own creations and exclusive property, they are "ours," I believe, only in sacred trust. And as new ways evolve whereby the dog comes to satisfy more varied human needs and interests, our indebtedness to the canine species increases accordingly.

   We owe our dogs so much; we owe it to them to read this book so that they too will enjoy a more satisfying relationship—one that this book can help us all realize and enjoy.

Dr. Michael W. Fox, Vice President
The Humane Society of the United States
2100 L Street, N.W.
Washington, D.C. 20037

PART ONE

FINDING YOUR BEST FRIEND

CHAPTER 1

Why Do You Want a Dog?

Two OUT OF FIVE U.S. families have at least one dog. Statistics show that Americans are buying more dogs and spending more money on them than ever before. For instance, in 1980 there were 46.1 million family-owned dogs in the United States. By 1986, this number had increased to 51.6 million. In 1980, dog owners spent $2.6 billion on dog food, and only five years later, that amount had increased to $3.1 billion.

Why are dogs suddenly so popular? Recently, two major factors have caused the above figures to soar. One is medical research indicating that pet ownership reduces tension, blood pressure, and the incidence of heart attacks. In other words, people who own dogs live longer. The second is the increase in break-ins and burglaries, which creates the need for protection; many homeowners look to dogs to provide this protection.

To find the right pet for the right reasons, a prospective dog owner needs guidance in order to prevent the unsuccessful choices that so frequently lead to homeless dogs and needless canine euthanasia. People interested in owning a dog must figure out why they want one: to provide affection, companionship, status, exercise, protection, baby-sitting, sociability, service, or good health? Parents have different needs; many believe that having a dog gives their children more emotional security and a sense of responsibility. The prospective pet owner benefits by first understanding his or her need for a dog.

Dogs offer one a sense of ideal love. By their warm physical presence and responsiveness to human contact, they give their owners a feeling of emotional security that is often missing from human relationships under the stress of daily living. Dogs can be a consistent source of warmth, trust, and unconditional love. For example, they can connect us to the blissful feelings of infancy when our mothers offered us these same caring qualities. Combining child-hood experiences with canine companionship creates a renewal of the human/animal bond.

GOING BACK TO CHILDHOOD TO SELECT YOUR CANINE

Not everyone grows up in a house with dogs. There is certainly no reason to expect emotional trauma in a dogless family. But those adults who did have a treasured pet often look back to happy memories that included this devoted friend. Others may regret never having had the pet they always wanted, since a dog is often a symbol of the "complete" family. However minimal your contact with dogs was as a child, the fact that you want one now virtually assures that you *did* form early impressions about dogs. Whatever the motivation, getting in touch with those early feelings is the first step toward making the right choice in adulthood.

Taking a risk—bringing something new into your life—always begins with a dream or an image. These early emotional yearnings are sketched in childhood before the onset of logical decision-making. The nourishing picture of reaching out to a responsive canine friend stays in the brain and, just like information stored on a computer, it can be retrieved at will. How can you get in touch with these memories and use them to help you identify your ideal dog? How can you then match this dream to the puppies and dogs that await you?

"When I think of the house I grew up in, I can see Lucky, my black cocker spaniel, lying on the foot of my bed and keeping me company. The bedroom never felt dark and I was not afraid when he was there." Tina (all names have been changed), a busy twenty-eight-year-old interior designer, sat in my office using childhood memories to begin her process of choosing a new dog. She had considered the traditional routes—looking in the newspaper or going to the pound—when her search began. But she decided that this time she wanted to recreate her childhood picture of the perfect dog companion. In other words, she was using creative imagery to help her make an intelligent choice.

"Lucky was always ready to play when I came home from school," Tina continued. She then explained that both of her parents worked, but her four-footed "baby-sitter" kept the loneliness at bay and helped her feel loved. When she decided the time was right for owning a dog, her excursions into her child-hood helped her narrow down her choices. She decided she wanted a dog that she could walk after work and that would help her turn off the stress from her daily battles—just as Lucky had helped her forget her loneliness. Tina then pulled out a large drawing pad and started to draw a picture of Lucky. This sketch went into her "dog file." The little cocker had been her first love, and recreating that image would help her understand the look of the dog she wanted as an adult. (Those less artistically inclined may get the same result simply by closing their eyes and remembering their special dog as vividly as possible.)

Aileen had wanted a dog of her own, but her mother always said no. As a thirty-two-year-old single woman, she went into therapy to help overcome her feelings of insecurity and lack of love. During our sessions, Aileen was forced to remember her mother saying no to a number of things she wanted or needed. Aileen realized that her main reason for wanting a dog was a need to nurture and take care of it in a way that she felt was missing in her own family relationships. All through her teen years, Aileen never gave up her dream of owning a dog. Today, she has a chocolate Labrador retriever, Pfeiffer. With Pfeiffer, Aileen is reexperiencing her childhood as she wishes it had been. She feels important and needed. Pfeiffer's love helps her reach out and, with this abundance of love, Aileen feels comfortable enough with herself to help others. Saturdays, she accompanies children with Down's syndrome to the zoo where they learn about loving and caring for animals. Aileen gives these youngsters the love that she feels she missed as a child. Pfeiffer always accompanies Aileen on these trips; he sits in the back seat of the car with the children.

COUPLES: COMBINING YOUR CHILDHOOD EXPERIENCES TO PICK THE RIGHT DOG

Ralph and Cheryl had just moved from a city condominium to a home in the suburbs. Even before the new lawn was finished, they began talking about getting a puppy. As they described their early experiences with dogs to me, I could see that finding a compatible dog would be a challenge. As children, their dog experiences were quite different. Ralph grew up near a lake. Bear, his male Newfoundland, had been the perfect companion for an active country boy who loved to swim and fish. As a result, Ralph tried to convince Cheryl that a "Bear" would be the perfect dog for them. But Cheryl didn't want a large, long-haired dog. She had grown up with Toby, a beagle mix, and wanted a dog small enough to hold. She showed me an old album with faded photographs showing Toby asleep on her bed. Cheryl then explained that she had been one of three sisters but that Toby had loved her the most. Cheryl wanted to renew that feeling of specialness by finding another "Toby."

Luckily, Cheryl and Ralph were both agreeable people and they decided to compromise. They filled out separate Dog History Forms (see below), and then shared their ideal dog dreams with each other. Eventually, they chose a bearded collie; it was active enough to satisfy Ralph's yen for an outdoor dog, yet loving enough to sit quietly beside Cheryl. Being open and listening to each other's childhood experiences enabled them to come up with a compromise. In the process, Ralph and Cheryl learned more about each other and were able to choose a dog that could fit both of their dreams.

IF YOUR DOG WAS YOUR HERO

George grew up in southwest London, spending his week's allowance on Saturday movie matinees. His first hero was the superdog Rin Tin Tin, the fearless Alsatian (the British term for a German shepherd) who swam rivers, saved babies, and performed other acts of daring. When George was ten, he took five carefully saved shillings and went to Club Row, an open-air market that sold puppies. There, George chose his first dog, a pure silver Alsatian with wonderful "stand-up" ears whom he named Rinny. George thought he had bought a male puppy but found out later, when his mother examined it, that Rinny was a female! Despite the mix-up, Rinny won George's heart. "I used to walk along the Thames with her. She was so smart. She taught herself how to heel without a leash. Idolizing Rin Tin Tin and later personifying that idolatry with my very own dog gave me enough confidence to change the world." As an adult, George settled in California. He shared this boyhood experience with his wife, who had never been allowed to have a dog and was touched by the influence George's dog hero had on him. Eventually, they purchased an enormous German shepherd pup, Noble Von Kuperhof. George was able to continue his childhood dream and his wife and son felt protected by this regal, intelligent animal.

REMEMBERING YOUR DOG AS FOUR-FOOTED THERAPIST

Sometimes the decision to select a specific type of dog is predicated on more than just hero worship. Carol, a high school teacher, had been in therapy with me for two years. During this time, she remarried and moved to a rustic home in a canyon. When talk of dog ownership began, the newlyweds found themselves at odds. As a child, her new husband John had owned a lovable mixed-breed terrier named Hector. But this was not the type of dog that Carol wanted. Carol needed John to understand how important her first dog had been to her. She told him that she adopted Noah, a long-haired collie, after her parents moved her from a progressive school to a more academic one in second grade. Carol's grades had dropped and she was beginning to feel like a failure. When Noah entered her life, Carol's schoolwork suddenly seemed easier and her grades went from Ds to Bs.

It was obvious to me from reading Carol's responses to the Dog History Form that she felt protected and secure in the presence of a large male dog. When John read Carol's form, he learned how Noah had helped to increase his wife's feelings of self-esteem and confidence, which laid the groundwork for her decision to become a teacher. He acquiesced to her desires and they selected a lovable Great Pyrenees whom they called Charlemagne.

SELECTING A DOG YOU IDENTIFY WITH

Some dog owners select a dog—either consciously or unconsciously—that shares their personality traits. This often makes the owner feel more secure. On the other hand, some dog owners select a canine that possesses characteristics they admire or would like to cultivate in themselves. These people may find it easier to talk about a dog's beauty, strengths, or unique personality than to talk about their own. In these cases, selecting a dog often helps bring out hidden attributes—such as warmth or social skills—in the owner.

Marybell has a two-year-old miniature schnauzer, Michael. "I love these dogs. They are independent and stubborn, just as I have always been! I like people with minds of their own and that goes for my dogs, too. In fact, I have acute hearing, just like my schnauzer." Marybell, a diminutive and extroverted lady, grew up with terriers and loved what she describes as their "strong egos." She says, "They always know what they want and they are determined to get it. When I first started my photocopying business, I had a few doubts about making it on my own, but Michael was my inspiration. Nothing was impossible for him. He'd undertake any challenge whatsoever, whether it was making it to the top of a steep canyon or holding his own with a larger dog. I kept getting the message from him that determination was the answer and now the business supports me *and* my dog show habit!"

Helen, on the other hand, selected a dog with personality traits different from her own and used her dog to draw her into new experiences. She had been a first grade teacher but gave up her career to marry and have a family. Her two sons grew up with several mixed-breed terriers, but the sons went off to college and the pets eventually died. Widowed at age fifty-two, Helen found herself growing more introverted and less eager to try new experiences. Her sons talked her into adopting a dog, thinking it would provide some much-needed companionship. She went to the animal shelter and found an alert three-month-old sheltie, Sandy, who was friendly, smart, and eager to please. Encouraged by these traits, Helen enrolled Sandy in dog obedience school. They started with an eight-week puppy training course. The experience was so novel—and so rewarding—for Helen that she decided to continue. They moved on to beginning and then novice classes. When Sandy was fifteen months old, he and Helen entered obedience competitions and successfully completed the three trials (with a high score). Soon, Sandy had a Companion Dog degree and Helen was as proud of her dog as she had been of her sons' college degrees! Helen enjoyed being a member of the local obedience club and Sandy lived up to his potential. Both received lots of attention and many rewards for their work. Helen is the first to admit that Sandy's outgoing personality is what spurred her in this new direction. She credits her pet with pulling her out of the doldrums and into a new and involving experience.

Sometimes a person's motivation for owning a pet is not healthy, as was the case with Bob. This young man left home at eighteen after a stormy adolescence. Bob had a lot of unresolved anger—aimed not only at his parents but at his friends too. They considered the "macho" image important and they constantly ridiculed Bob for his seeming lack of machismo. At this point, Bob decided to adopt a pit bull; he thought that this breed—which some view as extremely masculine—would impress his friends. However, Bob had neither the time nor the desire to train this dog properly. Left alone in the daytime, Attila howled constantly and chewed up furniture, shoes, and clothing. Obviously, the puppy was lonely and calling out for attention. On top of that, Bob found that owning this strong breed of dog did not affect his popularity; his friends did not view him any differently than before and he still had to struggle to develop his own identity. He found a home for the dog and entered therapy to try to solve his problems.

A dog relationship can nurture children's emotional growth and heal disappointments. When people recall their childhood memories and attitudes about dogs, the imprint of their "dog dream" comes clear: warm, tender, cared-for feelings, bold, brave, heroic memories, a powerful sense of security—whatever the image, it reveals the emotional needs behind the adult's choice of canine.

When the time comes to own a dog, calling up your childhood memories will help you make the right choice. Filling out the Dog History Form (opposite) helps bring back these memories. Record the details on a form, look at photos of your past canines, and even draw pictures of your memories. These steps help you make the right dog choice. If you have never owned a dog, or cannot think of one specific dog to concentrate on, don't worry. The following chapters will describe alternate methods.

DOG HISTORY FORM

Begin with your earliest dog memory. This may have been your own dog or a friend's or even a fictional dog that was important to you or one you thought about. Now, answer the following questions.

1. How old were you when you first encountered the dog?
2. What was the dog's name and age?
3. How many years did you spend together?
4. What was the dog's type, size, and hair color?
5. How was this dog selected?
6. Who named the dog? Was there any special meaning to the name?
7. Who fed it and exercised it?
8. What was your favorite play activity with it?
9. How was the dog trained? What training method was most effective?
10. Did the dog know any special tricks?
11. List one-word images and feelings that you associate with this dog.
12. What is your last memory of this dog?
13. In looking back, was it a good relationship or do you have mainly bad memories?
14. Do you think having a similar canine would be beneficial? Why or why not?

Now that you have learned some of the reasons for your wanting a dog, let's see if this is the right time for you to add one to your life.

CHAPTER 2

Are You Ready for a Dog?

ONCE THE DECISION to obtain a dog has been made, it is important to ask yourself this question: Are you ready? In the excitement of getting a dog, this consideration is often overlooked. When this happens, both dog and owner suffer. It is quite likely that the owners of the eighteen million dogs needlessly destroyed in the U.S. each year did not take the time to contemplate this issue, did not choose the right time in their lives to own a dog or did not psychologically prepare themselves for owning the dog they chose. Acquiring a new canine is similar to having a baby in that it brings both joy and stress to the household. In fact, potential dog owners could benefit from a "psychological pregnancy" which would prepare them for this new family member. In other words, you must be realistic about the cost, the time, and the energy necessary for dog rearing, or you will end up frustrated and disappointed. Your new dog could live with you for fifteen years or more, so it is important to stop and consider if that is really what you want and if you are prepared for this kind of commitment.

One couple, Gary and Ann, did not take this preparation step before they brought home their new puppy. While vacationing in the mountains, this couple purchased a six-week-old Newfoundland–black Labrador retriever mix. He was the largest in the litter of six furry pups being sold outside the local supermarket. Ann named him Buster.

"I took one look at those large black eyes and those enormous feet and I fell in love. Gary wanted a female because he'd heard they take less time to train, but Buster pushed the other pups aside and found us. So we called our landlady and talked her into letting us have a dog."

Gary took over the story from this point. "He was rebellious from the start. Because we both work full-time, we didn't have that much time to devote to his training. As a result, he was difficult to housebreak. And because we weren't home that much, he took his anger out on us by chewing everything in sight!"

Ann continued, "Now, he's five and we love him, but we have often had second thoughts about him and certainly we learned a lot about how to make this type of decision." Ann described in detail the horrors of Buster's first month. "Aside from chewing, he terrorized the cat, stole food off the counter, dug holes in the lawn, and broke through the living room window to chase a passing dog!" Despite two courses in obedience training, Buster remained difficult. He had several biting incidents, after which their veterinarian recommended he be neutered. There was some improvement afterwards, but the most helpful change came when they hired a dog behavioral specialist and both the owners and the pet changed their behavior.

In retrospect, several things went wrong in the acquisition of this dog. Certainly, Ann and Gary had not taken the time to consider carefully the pros and cons of owning a dog. In addition, selecting a puppy without seeing the mother dog or knowing something about her litter history is taking a gamble on the dog's future behavior. (The contrast between the black fluffy puppy with big paws and wonderful eyes and the strong-willed adolescent dog was amazing.) Neither Gary nor Ann was prepared for the time and leadership needed for dog training. By the time I met him at age five, Buster had settled down and his new trainer had taught his family how to alter some of his canine habits. But this was a long five years and a hard lesson for Ann and Gary.

RECOGNIZING THE WRONG TIME

All dogs need food, exercise, playtime, proper health care, and companionship. Training a dog requires time from each family member. Puppies in particular are very dependent on their owners, just as infants are on their mothers. Bringing up a puppy offers emotional rewards, but there are many hours involved in the early training. It takes time for these canine youngsters to become housebroken and to learn the rules of the house and yard. If this initial learning program is not planned in advance, the adorable puppy can become a monster dog, causing property damage and learning bad habits. The owners are then easily disenchanted. At this point, some dogs are returned to their original owners or, worse yet, sent to the pound. Such a failure is a negative experience for children and a poor emotional start for the dog. Even if not doomed to an early death, the dog can develop psychological problems. The child may well learn that it's okay to go back on commitments and shirk responsibility. Being realistic about planning for the time involved in dog owning and training can help prevent an unhappy ending to the dream of a family dog.

Some people get a puppy for the right reasons but at the wrong time. Bill and Irene owned a five-year-old female Rottweiler, Becky, and a neutered male Afghan hound, Beasley. When Beasley died, Becky was visibly lonesome and disheartened. Irene, who was two months pregnant, decided that it would be nice to get a puppy who could grow with the new baby. They chose a male Rottweiler, not only to provide companionship for Becky but also to show. They carefully researched the breeders and selected an outgoing male with show potential. They wanted both dogs to be ready for the new baby, so when Irene was six months pregnant she enrolled the new pup, Bogart, in obedience training while Bill took Becky for a refresher course. But as the pregnancy advanced, Irene had less energy for training Bogart. Without regular sessions, he became restless and, missing the attention he was used to, he tested his new mistress constantly. They hired a weekly trainer for Bogart, but without daily practice the pup was still a handful for Irene. Finally they were forced to make a difficult decision: When the baby was one month old, they tearfully returned Bogart to the breeder. Luckily, they *had* researched breeders thoroughly; this was one who put the dog's welfare first, and thus agreed to take him back.

It became obvious that although they had selected the dog they felt was right for them, they had neglected to weigh all the factors involved in dog ownership, and one of them—adequate time—did not exist, thus the failed experience.

CAN YOU AFFORD A DOG?

Another factor to consider before you make the decision to own a dog is money. According to a National Animal Control Association survey conducted in 1985 (as reported in the New York Erie County S.P.C.A. Newsletter in December 1985), there is a definite relationship between the amount of money paid for an animal and the emotional commitment the owner feels toward that animal. The table below reveals the results of this study:

Cost of Dog	Length of Ownership
Over $100	36 months average
$50 to $99	33 months average
$10 to $49	24 months average
Less than $10	28 months average
Free	17 months average

As one can see, getting a pet for free does not seem to make for a long-term relationship. Potential dog owners must realize that the cost of purchasing a dog is only the first part of the financial responsibility involved. The

Humane Society of the United States informs us that the biggest cost in caring for a dog is food, followed by veterinary care. In 1986, according to the Pet Food Institute (the national trade association of dog and cat food manufacturers), $3.1 million was spent on dog food. This means you can expect to pay anywhere from $200 to $600 a year for a single dog. Of course, the amount and kind of food that dogs require depends on their size, age, activity, and lifestyle (showing, breeding, amount of exercise).

In addition, your dog budget will include a yearly license fee (lower for altered dogs), grooming equipment and/or professional grooming, bowls, and toys. And, if you have a puppy, you'll need new collars as the dog grows, a leash, and a crate for housebreaking (see Chapter Eight, "Educating Your Dog"). Also, maintaining the warm weather battle against fleas can include buying everything from flea sprays, powders, and baths for the dog to flea bombs for the home. Some breeds are prone to flea allergy and will require veterinary care and medicine. During vacation and travel, dog-sitting or boarding costs must be considered. If you do not have a fenced yard, you may be looking at new fencing costs (or run the risk of losing your canine). All these costs should be budgeted *before* you acquire your new dog.

HEALTH CARE

Maintaining a healthy dog requires good veterinary care. Responsible pet owners, like responsible parents, know the value of quality health care. Puppies need vaccinations against life-threatening diseases such as canine distemper, viral hepatitis, leptospirosis, parvovirus, and rabies. And, like children, dogs need these vaccinations kept up to date. Another initial cost incurred is spaying or neutering, which may add years to a pet's life. (Tumors occur quite frequently in older dogs that have not been altered.) As your dog grows older and geriatric problems occur, regular medical checkups become even more important. A healthy dog is well worth this time and care, but a new owner must be aware of the costs involved.

DOG-SITTING—A REHEARSAL FOR PET OWNERSHIP

One way to help you decide if you are ready for the commitment to canine ownership is dog-sitting a friend's pet. It would be doubly helpful if you could find both the sex and breed you expect to get; the dog-sitting experience will then give you the opportunity to see how the specific dog would fit into your life. Naturally, all puppies and dogs have their own unique personalities and you will have only a glimpse of the future family picture. But the experience can help you see what some of the changes in your normal routine would be.

Mike and Carrie, a couple in their late twenties, were thinking of starting a family and thought that a puppy would give them a taste of parenthood. They were avid skiers and had been considering a cold-weather breed, like the Alaskan malamute, which they thought might enjoy the snow with them. They persuaded one of their friends to lend them his handsome six-month-old pup, Jambo, for a ski weekend. Jambo was right at home in the snow and cold. The tryout was well worth the effort. The following month, Mike and Carrie confidently selected a seven-week-old malamute pup of their own.

GETTING THE FAMILY READY

Everyone in the family should be involved in choosing and preparing for the new dog. Before the selection is made, talk about the various breeds and about the amount of care your new pet will require. Like the puppy-sitting exercise, a family conference can help you to explore the fears and potential problems which may arise with dog ownership. Training a new puppy requires honest, open communication between care-givers. Don't wait until *after* you get your dog to find out that someone feels it's too much work or has reservations about the breed or size.

Brent and Karen had different attitudes about the choice of a Rhodesian Ridgeback puppy. Brent fell in love with the breed while filming a movie in Kenya. At six feet, four inches tall, he identified instantly with the power and size of the Ridgeback. He watched several of them fearlessly protect their owner and, when he returned to the States, started looking for this handsome but rare breed. Unfortunately, Karen had never told him that she was bitten by a large dog as a child and had been afraid of them ever since. They came to me to work out Karen's problem so Brent could get the Ridgeback. We worked out a plan to help Karen relearn her experience with dogs. One step was that after each of Karen's sessions with me, she and Brent would visit dog orphans at the local humane society. Brent would find the friendliest puppy and they would take it outside its cage and play with it. Karen first started playing with small dogs and gradually increased the size each week. Then they audited several obedience training sessions so Karen could get a feeling for how to control dogs of every size. During this time, Karen made friends with my Rottweiler, Lorelei, who came to the office and acted as my cotherapist. Lorelei is a gentle, affectionate dog, and Karen came to like and trust her despite her size and strength. After five months of carefully planned relearning, Karen was ready to test out her own Rhodesian Ridgeback puppy. She and Brent chose a sweet, outgoing female whom they named Honey. By gaining control of her fear, Karen prepared herself to live happily with her new canine.

PREPARING YOURSELF FOR YOUR NEW DOG

When you begin to consider owning a dog, a Dog File is the perfect place to keep your thoughts about it, as well as information about different breeds. During this selection time, make a habit of jotting down ideas about how a dog will fit into your life. Also keep information about dog organizations breeders, dog shows, and dogs you meet and like or those you are not particularly attracted to. Another exercise is for each family member to prepare a script which includes a new family dog. Have each person write a scenario showing how your life would change once a puppy or dog is introduced. The following Readiness Quiz will help you formulate your answers.

READINESS QUIZ

1. Where would the dog sleep and eat?

2. How many hours would it be alone? How would it get out of the house when it needed to?

3. Who would feed and exercise it?

4. How would it get along with any pets you have now?

5. Who would take it to the veterinarian?

6. If you choose a puppy, who would be responsible for housetraining it?

7. If you go away on a trip, where would it stay?

Next, the entire family should share their scripts and answers about the care of the new dog and see if they are in agreement. If not, you will need to spend some time talking before you go any further in the selection process. Open, honest communication about owning a new dog lays the groundwork for a successful relationship.

Evaluating how the dog will fit into your family's lifestyle saves pain and disappointment for both you and the dog. Once the family is in agreement about the finer points of dog ownership, you will be ready to look at the kind of dog that best suits your needs.

CHAPTER 3

The Dog
You Need Now

O NCE YOU HAVE DECIDED that you are ready for a dog, how do you know what kind will suit your lifestyle? Surveys show that pet owners consider companionship the number one reason for acquiring a dog. The truth is that dog owners really want more. Many couples acquire a dog as a playmate for their child; some need a dog for protection; single people often select dogs that are athletic and can join them in various outdoor activities. No matter how much you want to own a dog or how well you understand the responsibilities involved, your choice will never work if you and the dog are irreconcilably mismatched from the beginning.

The first step is to know yourself. If you are a single person, your choice will be easier: You select the dog *you* want, considering the reasons *you* feel are most important. If you are married and/or have children, there are more factors involved. Before you start looking at prospective pets, sit down with your family members and talk.

Dog ownership is an important step, much like home ownership. Most people go about selecting a new home with great care. They look at the neighborhood, the original cost, the upkeep involved; generally they imagine themselves living in it for a long time. They would do well to treat selecting a new dog with the same care. In many cases, a dog may stay in your life longer than you will stay in a new home; it is necessary to make a thorough assessment of your needs and life situation as they pertain to the canine. Setting up a section in your Dog File called "Need Assessment" is an efficient way to define your needs and your family's priorities so that you can match the kinds of dogs available to your needs and desires.

DEFINING YOUR NEEDS

Different breeds of dogs have a wide range of personality characteristics. Different size families have different needs for a dog. Surveys suggest that in most families the mother feeds and cares for the dog. But anyone can take on this responsibility and enjoy it. Thinking about how the new dog will fit into your life helps you define a satisfying role for it.

The Need Assessment Exercise should be done with all the members of your family, since each individual has specific needs for a new canine companion. Give each person a chance to respond to each question; only an open forum will allow a successful choice to be made.

THE NEED ASSESSMENT EXERCISE

A. *Personality*—One of the first considerations is how a new dog will fit into your family; you must therefore consider its personality—how it matches your activities, your home, and your lifestyle.

1. Who is going to spend the most time with the dog and what activities will be shared with it?

2. Do you want a dog that is playful and demands attention or one that is quiet and independent?

3. Will your dog be mainly indoors or outdoors?

4. Will you be away for long hours during the day and expect the dog to be fairly quiet in your absence?

5. Do you have close neighbors and are you concerned about their being annoyed by barking?

6. Do you live in an apartment or a house? How large is your yard?

7. Do you want a dog that is friendly and easily accepts your friends?

8. Does your family engage in recreational activities, such as camping, skiing, hunting, fishing, going to the beach, and so on? Do you want your dog to accompany you?

B. *Appearance*—The look of a dog is a major factor for many. Some like a large, solid dog; others melt at the thought of picking up a long-haired bundle of fur.

1. Do you want a large, medium, or small dog?

2. Do you want a long-haired dog that will require grooming and, if so, who will be responsible for this chore?

    3. If you are considering a very large dog, are you aware that they do not live as long as smaller breeds?

    4. Do you prefer a cuddly lap dog or a large dog that is not necessarily built to be held?

C. *Exercise*—Exercising your dog is a wonderful shared activity and is healthy for both you and the dog. All dogs require exercise but some, because of their inherited skills, have a higher need to run. If they do not get the kind of exercise they were bred for, they can develop health and behavioral problems.

    1. Do you enjoy taking long walks and expect your dog to accompany you?

    2. Do you want your canine to be a running companion? Are you aware that vigorous running requires that your dog have a certain physique?

    3. Do you want a dog that needs minimal exercise?

D. *Training*—Training improves the owner-dog relationship and gives a dog boundaries and emotional security. The right kind of training leads to a well-adjusted dog. But some dogs are easier to train than others.

    1. Who will take the major responsibility for training your new dog?

    2. Is it important that you have an easy-to-train dog?

    3. If you are able to be the "pack leader" for your dog, do you feel confident enough to train a dominant, strong-willed dog?

    4. Are you considering entering the dog in obedience competitions?

E. *Children*—Not all dogs are appropriate for every age child, so try to involve your children in the selection of the family dog as much as possible to avoid any complications.

    1. If your children are the main reason for acquiring a dog, when will they play with it, exercise it, and help care for it?

    2. Do you want a dog who is primarily a playmate for your child?

F. *Protection*—The need for a watchdog and protector is another reason people adopt a new dog. But sometimes a good watchdog can bring unthought-of problems.

    1. Is home protection one of the major reasons that you want a dog?

2. Do you want a dog that will bark and alert you to strangers, regardless of how your neighbors feel?

3. Do you have fussy neighbors who would complain at the softest
bark?

4. Are you willing to invest time and money in training a protection
· dog?

5. Are you willing to deal with the problems and legal complications which may result from bites or other types of attacks?

G. *Special Needs*—Many dogs provide guidance and companionship to
physically handicapped, emotionally disabled, or blind or deaf persons. But, again, there are some considerations to be taken into
account.

1. Is there anyone at home with physical handicaps that requires a
dog with special skills?

2. Are there any elderly persons (who might be easily overwhelmed
by a large, high-spirited dog) living with you, or do they visit
frequently?

3. Do you have the commitment (time and money) necessary to
train the dog to suit your special needs?

H. *Other Considerations*
Male or Female—In some breeds, the females are more easily trained
and controlled than males. Unless you plan to breed them, females
should be spayed. Until a female is spayed, she will come into heat
about twice a year; this attracts numerous male dogs to your home.
Generally, males are more likely to roam if they are not living within
securely fenced boundaries. Some male dogs are aggressive toward
other male dogs and this would require a strong hand during walks.
Before you begin to look at dogs, it is wise to have a gender preference already in your mind.

1. Do you plan to spay your female/neuter your male?

2. Do you plan to breed your dog?

3. Do you plan to show your dog?

Age—Owning a puppy is fun and provides a lot of challenge. But
housetraining and educating puppies takes time and patience. In addition, they need frequent meals and attention. They are great chewers and can destroy slippers and furniture and, like restless children,
are likely to get into trouble when you are not there to supervise. An
adult dog is usually housetrained and has established habits which

may be good or bad. With an adult dog, what you see in looks and disposition is what you get. (If you opt for an adult dog, obedience training is still recommended, so that it will know that you are in charge.)

1. Do you have the time and interest to train a young puppy?

2. Are you interested in taking obedience training classes?

3. Would you be patient in housetraining, which will involve much cleaning up of floors and rugs?

4. Who in the family will be responsible for training?

Adding to your Canine Family—You may already have a dog and are considering adding another to your household. For example, when my Rottweiler Lorelei was four, I decided to get another Rottweiler puppy because I missed having a puppy in the house and I wanted to give Lorelei some company. I also believed that a puppy would keep Lorelei young and playful. My conjectures turned out to be true. But before you make a decision about a second dog, you must consider that two dogs require more time and attention; they need twice as much food, twice as many baths, and double the veterinary care and exercise. (However, when it comes to play, I discovered a bonus: My younger dog encourages the older one to exercise and the two of them play constantly.) As a rule, a mix of genders—one male, one female—is preferable. The least favorable combination is two males.

1. Do you have the time and space for more than one dog?

2. Who will care for the new one?

3. Who will care for the first dog?

DISCUSSING YOUR RESPONSES

You and your family must now discuss your answers. You may think of other needs. There may be some answers you do not agree on. Be sure to discuss them in your family conference. Keep your Need Assessment Exercise in your Dog File and refer to it as your family gets closer to making a final decision.

WHERE TO LEARN MORE

Your Dog File now contains a Dog History Form, pictures of dogs that you owned or liked, and the Need Assessment Exercise. The next step toward successful dog ownership is twofold: You must first read about different breeds in dog magazines and books and then talk to experts (veterinarians, obedience trainers) and other dog owners. Research is the key to selecting the right dog from the hundreds of mixed-breed orphans and purebred dogs that are available.

BOOKS THAT WILL HELP

Almost every year, a new guidebook is published which describes American Kennel Club breeds. It is illustrated with pictures of over 120 breeds of dogs which are recognized and shown in this country. A number of authorities in the field have published books about the temperament and behavior of some of these breeds.

Outstanding among these is a book written by two veterinarians from the University of California at Davis, Benjamin and Lynette Hart. Their book, entitled *The Perfect Puppy: How to Choose Your Dog by Its Behavior* (New York: W. H. Freeman and Company, 1988), describes the behavioral characteristics of fifty-six breeds of AKC dogs. Using ratings from forty-seven veterinarians and forty-eight obedience judges, the Harts created breed profiles which describe how these dogs would act in various situations. By looking at these profiles, the reader can see how these dogs compare in such traits as excitability, barking, playfulness, obedience training, aggression toward other dogs, dominance over owner, territorial defense, demand for affection, and behavior around children. In addition to the profiles, the book contains "clusters" which describe dogs of a similar nature but of different sizes and with different aptitudes. For instance, you may decide you like the profile of a Labrador retriever because it's an ideal family dog and easy to train. But you may eliminate this breed because Labradors are not good watchdogs. You need only to follow the cluster suggestion to look for a similar dog—like a collie—which has all the same pluses as the Labrador but which would be better for home protection. Or maybe you want a family dog with even less tendency to bark than a collie. The cluster research would lead you to a golden retriever.

This book would be a valuable addition to your Dog File. The information presented in *Perfect Puppy* is well researched, easy to understand, and well worth reading. Of course, keep in mind that there are individual differences within any breed. In addition, home environment and training are as important as breed differences.

Another book worth a look is *The Right Dog for You*, by animal psychologist Daniel Tortora, Ph. D. (New York: Fireside Books/Simon and Schuster, 1980). It describes 110 dog breeds in terms of size, activity level, tendency to dominate, sociability, learning ability, and aptitude for becoming a guard dog. Dr. Tortora has studied canine behavior and gives a detailed description of each breed, with a special emphasis on potential problem behavior.

A Celebration of Dogs (New York: Times Books, 1982) by Roger Caras is another important resource. This is a warm, humorous, well-written book that combines Caras's extensive experience in dog ownership with a description of many dog breeds and their histories and personalities.

MAGAZINES TO LOOK FOR

Dogs USA (and its sister publication, *Dogs Canada*) is a beautifully illustrated annual magazine. Contributing writers are usually authors who have published works on different facets of dog life. The magazine contains a number of excellent color photos of different breeds and a breed directory for the United States (and for Canada in *Dogs Canada*).

Dog World is a monthly magazine with useful information about shows for conformation and obedience training. (In the conformation competition, each dog is judged against the standard of perfection for its breed. After the championships, champions are bred together to ensure that the ideal is maintained.) This publication also contains articles about dog health, history, and behavior. At the back of the magazine is an extensive list of U. S. breeders. (This is a good place to get telephone numbers and addresses to find the breed of your choice.)

Dog Fancy is also a monthly magazine. It contains useful, informative articles and columns which offer advice on bringing up a healthy, happy dog. One dog breed is featured each month; if this breed is one you are considering, be sure to keep the issue for your Dog File.

GOING TO THE DOGS!

Now you are ready! You have looked at your reasons for acquiring a dog and understand the responsibilities involved. You have collected your Dog History Form, Readiness Quiz, and Need Assessment Exercise in your Dog File. You may also have added a book or some magazines to the file. You have read about the breeds that interest you. In other words, you're fully prepared to take the plunge! This is the time to start looking at dogs in your neighborhood and asking owners about them. This is an easy process because most dog owners enjoy talking about their dogs. Of course, as with proud parents, there may be some prejudice or exaggeration, but the information should still be helpful. Another excellent source, particularly if you already have a dog, is your veterinarian. He or she is well qualified to give you information on potential health problems. (For instance, if you are interested in getting a large dog to go running with you, it must have good hips and sound bone structure. If someone in your family is allergic to dog hair, you need to know about breeds that don't shed much.) Your vet deals with these issues daily and is a valuable resource.

In the chapters that follow, you will learn how to find the dog that's right for you, whether it is a lovable orphan, an endearing purebred, a dog for protection, a puppy for your children, or a dog with special skills.

CHAPTER 4

Adopting an Orphan

H OW CAN YOU DECIDE if adopting an orphan is
the right choice for you? And if you do adopt
one, how do you select the dog that is best suited to your needs? Rescuing an
orphan is a selfless, heartwarming thing to do. But facing a bevy of eager dogs
kept behind bars does not make that selection an easy one.

Sue and Danny Carroll were ready to get a new dog a little while after their
fourteen-year-old Sealyham terrier died. They decided they would like a larger
dog that would not remind them of their beloved terrier. Sue and her two
children visited the local shelter and fell in love at first sight with a young German shepherd mix. Two-year-old King was playful and also seemed well behaved. It looked like the perfect match and Sue adopted the dog that day.

However, when Danny greeted King at the door, things changed. Danny
approached King. The dog backed off and growled. Then the dog willingly
followed Sue into the back yard but wouldn't reenter the house while Danny
was there. Clearly the dog had negative associations with men. The next day
the Carrolls decided that King was not the right dog for the family. Luckily
they were able to return him and get a Lhasa apso which fit into the family
more comfortably.

With any dog selection, time and preparation are imperative. First of all,
all members of the family should visit the shelter to get a feeling for the dog.
Not only can you rule out canines unsuitable to the entire family, but this step
also involves everyone in the selection process, increasing each family member's commitment to the choice. Next, you must be prepared to gather as much
information about the adoptee as is available. (In some cases, the dogs are
strays and you will not have anything to go on except the behavioral evaluation

from the shelter.) Any information at all is valuable. If the previous dog owner has not provided a history, speak to the shelter employees and to the volunteers who walk the dogs or tend to them; these people have a wealth of information about the dogs in residence.

Most of the canines found in shelters are not puppies but young adult dogs who desperately need homes. They are almost all mixed-breed combinations, but, occasionally, you may be able to find a purebred. However, adopting a shelter dog is not for everyone. By taking the Dog Orphan Adoption Test, you can see how appropriate this move would be for you.

DOG ORPHAN ADOPTION TEST

Circle the number that best fits your feeling about each question.

	AGREE			DISAGREE	
	5	4	3	2	1

1. As a child, I always wanted to bring home stray animals.

        5   4   3   2   1

2. I enjoy a wide variety of different dog breeds.

        5   4   3   2   1

3. I have no interest in showing my dog in the breed ring. (To compete in the breed ring, a dog must have AKC registered papers, which is very rare for orphans.)

        5   4   3   2   1

4. I think adult dogs should be spayed or neutered to reduce the number of unwanted dogs in our community.

        5   4   3   2   1

5. I do not need to know the pedigree of my dog.

        5   4   3   2   1

6. I would prefer a dog that is over six months old.

        5   4   3   2   1

7. I do not want to breed my dog.

        5   4   3   2   1

8. I would like to do something to help homeless pets who might otherwise lose their lives.

        5   4   3   2   1

9. I am patient and could allow time for a dog to adjust to my home.

5   4   3   2   1

10. I feel that as a dog matures, its personality is even more interesting than when it was a puppy.

5   4   3   2   1

11. I think that mixed-breed dogs are as interesting as purebred dogs.

5   4   3   2   1

12. I have previously adopted a dog and was happy with it.

5   4   3   2   1

Total your score.

60 to 48 points—Your sensitivity and experience make you an ideal person to adopt an orphan dog.

47 to 36 points—You have a genuine interest in dog orphans but need to review your priorities in order to see if a shelter dog is what you want. Perhaps visiting a shelter and talking to the staff will help you decide.

35 points or less—You have serious reservations about adopting an orphan dog. More than likely, a purebred dog is what you want. Go to dog shows in your community and see the different breeds. In addition, talking and visiting with dog organizations in your community can give you more information about your best choice.

Although a high score is no guarantee of a successful adoption, it does show good potential for success in adopting an orphan dog.

WHERE TO FIND AN ORPHAN

There are over two thousand animal shelters in this country, and numerous pet organizations. All of them house homeless dogs. The first humane society, called the American Society for the Prevention of Cruelty to Animals (ASPCA), was formed in 1866 in New York by Henry Bergh, who became concerned about the treatment of work horses and the drowning of unwanted dogs. He wrote a Declaration of Rights of Animals which laid the foundation for the first anti-cruelty law written to protect animals. Today, humane societies and private nonprofit pet organizations across the country offer shelter to stray pets and give potential pet owners the opportunity to adopt a four-legged friend for life.

Generally shelter dogs come from one of three backgrounds: They are abused animals that have been rescued, street strays that are in need of food and housing, or dogs turned in by owners who can no longer keep them.

PROFILE:
RESCUED DOGS/PROSPECTIVE OWNERS

Kisha, a skinny three-year-old female greyhound, greeted me at the entrance of the Ventura Humane Society and cautiously rubbed her soft gray nose against my leg. Kisha was extremely thin and very ill when she was discovered, tied up and malnourished in a backyard pen. Now, after one month in the shelter, she has received veterinary care, a nutritious diet, and special attention from the entire staff of this friendly shelter in Ojai, California. I learned that her owner used her only during hunting season and ignored her the rest of the year; Kisha remained tied up, was given no opportunity to exercise, and had only the minimum amount of food and water to keep her alive. She was found by the humane society, nearly starved to death, on a tip from a concerned neighbor. At the shelter, Kisha had the run of the indoor area for several hours each day so she could learn to renew her trust in people. This "people" attention was preparing her for a new home with an owner who would treat her with love and kindness. So far, there are three families who have expressed an interest in adopting her.

For over 120 years, the humane societies in this country have responded to calls for help when informed that animals were being neglected or abused. As you may imagine, it is not always easy to find the right home for a trauma-tized dog. Abused animals are similar to abused children; they too need a sup-portive environment and lots of love. Prospective owners should have previous experience with dogs and the patience to work with the animal during its phys-ical and/or emotional convalescence. They must realize that adopting an abused dog can be rewarding, but it is not for everyone and most certainly should *not* be undertaken impulsively or simply as an act of kindness. It is even more important in this situation that every member of the family meet the dog and then carefully discuss the pros and cons of adopting it. Most of all, it's important to realize that rehabilitating abused animals requires more commit-ment than adopting one of the "normal" strays. If you do not have the time or emotion to commit to this pet, then it's best not to adopt it.

PROFILE:
REJECTED DOGS/PROSPECTIVE OWNERS

The majority of dogs found in shelters have been turned in by owners who, for some reason, cannot keep them. The most common reasons are behavioral (barking, chewing); some are personal (change in environment, divorce, ill-ness, children). Unfortunately, many canines end up in shelters because their owners did not have realistic expectations of what dog ownership entails. They selected the dog on impulse and then lost interest in it, or they failed to plan a training program that would control potential behavior problems. Prospective owners of rejected dogs must have enough patience to deal with behavioral problems. For example, dog obedience school may be necessary and the owner must be committed enough to undertake this experience. Most importantly, prospective owners of rejected dogs must fully understand the responsibilities involved in dog ownership. This is not a decision to be entered into lightly.

SHELTERS PLAY A ROLE IN SUCCESSFUL ADOPTIONS

When shelter workers see a dog adopted, they hope for a permanent place-ment. During research for this book, I visited many humane societies and city pounds; all of them routinely distribute educational pamphlets on health care, housetraining, nutrition, and behavioral training. All interview the potential owners and some even visit the prospective home. Some require a written agreement from the owner's landlord giving permission to keep a dog. If chil-dren under age six are involved, shelter workers often observe how well-behaved the children are and how they relate to the dog before the animal is actually adopted. Often, the shelter dog is released on a trial basis and if the adoption does not work, the animal is returned. All shelters have arrangements for either low-cost or free (depending on income) health evaluations for the adopted dog. Spaying or neutering is required before adoption. (If the animal is too young for this procedure at the time of adoption, arrangements are made to return a portion of the adoption fee when the dog is brought back for surgery.)

Shelters work very hard to place the right dog with the right family. For example, the Humane Society of Missouri has a "get acquainted room" which is covered with colorful animal paintings; this enables prospective owner and pet to "get acquainted" in a more private environment. The Riverside Humane Society in California has a fifteen-day trial period during which the adopted dog may be exchanged for another or returned altogether for a monetary re-fund. This humane society believes that you will know how an animal reacts to you only if it lives in your home.

The Animal Rescue League of Boston offers advice to pet owners who must give up their pets and describes the brief life of a dog living on the streets of Boston. The San Diego Humane Society uses an adoption questionnaire to evaluate the prospective dog owner's sense of responsibility and commitment. (The questionnaire asks the dog owner why he or she wants a dog, where he or she plans to keep it, and if he or she is prepared to provide medical care, grooming, proper diet, and exercise.) The Massachusetts SPCA not only offers initial health care at the Boston-based Angell Memorial Animal Hospital, but also gives pet owners canine toothbrushes and specially created animal toothpaste.

Educating the public about responsible pet care and animal population control is one of the most important parts of every shelter's program. The Los

Angeles SPCA has a traveling animal ambassador who lectures schoolchildren on these topics. Humane Educational Director Jane Evans and her adopted seven-year-old papillon mix, Ruggie, visit elementary schools, teaching and demonstrating what makes a good dog citizen and how children can become dependable pet owners.

THE SAN FRANCISCO HUMANE SOCIETY— A CAMELOT FOR DOGS

The San Francisco SPCA (SF/SPCA) is a model of the spirit of humane societies in this country. Not surprisingly, its pet adoption rate is 97 percent. The old gray building on 16th Street that houses the SF/SPCA offers stray canines food, medical care, and warm baths. All dogs receive vaccinations, a personality profile, and a large clean den in which to wait for their next home. After a dog is adopted, it might attend a "school" sponsored by the SF/SPCA or the master could call a hotline to obtain answers to any adjustment problems.

This shelter has made dog adoption successful and has helped meet the diverse needs of the citizens of San Francisco. How does this program work? From the building basement, which houses an 1890 SPCA horse ambulance, to the "penthouse," which contains a grooming college and a training center for hearing-ear dogs, the goal is always the same: to provide a caring alliance between humans and animals. According to Richard Avanzino, program director since 1976, "The adopters do not have to have a 'perfect home' for our dogs, which might otherwise be euthanized. What we really want is love and commitment and these don't depend on a beautiful home or a strong fence. The poor, the elderly, the physically and emotionally handicapped—all can offer our dogs the miracle of life."

Several weeks after a dog is adopted, the SF/SPCA sends a questionnaire to the owner, inquiring about the reason for adoption, the present physical and emotional state of the dog, and the quality of service that the adopting family received at the shelter. Answers indicate that many people come to the SF/SPCA because of the good selection of pets and are extremely satisfied with their adoptees. (One respondent who had just acquired a five-year-old male shepherd mix noted that this was the second dog from the shelter and both were "wonderful pets.")

Avanzino's feelings represent more than a humanistic dream of a better life for people and animals. For example, in 1987 the SF/SPCA, which is open twenty-four hours a day and seven days a week, adopted out 10,678 animals and reunited 1,841 lost pets with their owners. More than five hundred volunteers are trained to interview prospective pet owners and help them choose the right companion to fit their life. The Adoption Outreach program takes adoptable animals to community centers and screens and places them with responsible owners who cannot make it to the actual shelter. The Foster Care program calls on volunteer "parents" to provide loving care to injured or orphaned animals until these pets are adoptable. The SF/SPCA houses a Pet Grooming College which increases the dogs' chances for adoption, a well-groomed animal being more appealing than one which is not.

In addition, shelter instructors may be asked to give lectures to school-children on how animals live and grow. One of the major blocks to pet-owner compatibility is antisocial behavior. To combat this problem, the SF/SPCA staff and volunteers analyze the temperaments of abandoned animals and work with the dogs to make them more adoptable. Once the dog is placed, "trouble-shooting" classes and a telephone hotline help solve any ongoing problems. On-site medical treatment, and transportation if necessary, is offered free to senior citizen pet owners with limited incomes; free emergency care is given to stray animals. The Cinderella fund helps shelter animals that need extensive care, and then prepares them for placement.

However, the SF/SPCA does more than take exceptional care of orphaned animals and place them in good homes. They have found creative ways that dogs can serve the citizens of San Francisco. Community programs include the Animal-Assisted Therapy program, in which dogs visit or are placed with the seriously ill or disabled, convalescents, the elderly, and patients in hospitals and rehabilitation centers. The Hearing Dog program screens and selects animals, matches them with appropriate hearing-impaired persons, and provides train-ing for both.

Information on the humane society in your city can be obtained by con-tacting the Humane Society of the United States, 2100 L Street, N. W., Wash-ington, D. C. 20037; telephone (202) 452-1100.

OTHER OPTIONS

Adoptable dogs can also be found at one of the myriad local animal rescue groups around the country, many of which have been founded by concerned citizens. Like their counterparts the animal shelters, these nonprofit groups try to place dogs with caring and responsible owners and work to improve condi-tions for stray animals. For example, three Los Angeles–area organizations work hard on behalf of strays: Actors and Others for Animals not only places orphaned dogs in good homes, it also helps to educate prospective owners and sometimes offers financial assistance to owners with large veterinary bills. The Amanda Foundation performs last-day rescues of shelter animals that are scheduled to be put to sleep. In addition, it offers a health guarantee, vaccina-tions, and obedience lessons with a trainer in the new owner's home. Friends of Animals not only rescues and boards dogs until they can be adopted, but provides food for pets owned by low-income senior citizens and others in emergency situations. Volunteers also take dogs to convalescent hospitals and rest homes for therapeutic visits.

If you wish to adopt a dog from an animal organization in your community but do not know how to get in touch with one, a local veterinarian should be able to provide you with the information you need.

THE HELEN WOODWARD ANIMAL CENTER

This unusual nonprofit animal center in Rancho Santa Fe, California provides an attractive setting, attentive staff, and a short-term residence for orphaned dogs. The adoption center is located between the therapeutic riding horses and the animal treatment facility. Each prospective owner must fill out an extensive questionnaire. No one is allowed to acquire a pet without spending some hours thinking about the commitment involved and considering his or her ability to provide proper care to the adoptee.

Before an owner turns in a dog for adoption, he or she must fill out a six-page questionnaire describing the dog's previous housing, education, home behavior, relationship with people, and health and life history. The questionnaire ends by asking for the reason for surrender and then asks two more questions: (1) Is there any special problem about this dog that the center should know about which will enable them to place it most appropriately? (2) Are there any special comments you would like to make concerning this animal?

Before a dog is accepted, it must pass both physical and psychological examinations. These steps are taken in order to satisfy the center's plan to maintain a disease-free facility and to place only physically sound and psychologically well-adjusted animals.

Each dog is evaluated to determine its personality from the moment it moves into the kennel until it leaves with its new owner. Kennel technicians observe its acceptance of and behavior in confinement and watch for such problems as growling, fearfulness, bad reaction to male workers, relationship to other dogs, and acceptance of control by humans. They observe whether the dog howls in the kennel, is confident, aggressive, and/or responsive to commands. Lastly, they observe any change in behavior during a dog's stay in the kennels. Dogs that pass this evaluation along with the health check are eligible for adoption.

Adopting a dog from the center is even more rigorous than surrendering one to it. The eight-page adoption questionnaire begins with the statement, "It is quite true that not every person who desires to own a pet should own a pet." So warned, the adopter then must answer questions about the dog's future supervision and living arrangements; the adopter's previous experience with dog training; knowledge of dog nutrition, health, and grooming; and attitudes about spaying and neutering and dog discipline. The questionnaire ends with the questions, "What problems can you foresee in dog ownership?" and "What do you expect to gain from owning a dog?" As evidenced by its strict standards, this center is clearly working to prevent a mismatch or poorly made selection. Those who are willing to go through the rigorous application procedure have an excellent chance of ending up with a successful pet adoption.

ADOPTION GUIDELINES

Planning ahead, knowing your own needs, and obtaining the maximum amount of information about your new dog all increase your chances of a successful adoption.

Get out your Dog File and all your organized information. If your score on the Dog Orphan Test indicates that you are ready to adopt one, make a list of the animal groups in your community. You are now ready to begin the search for your new pet! The following procedure will help to ensure that everything goes smoothly.

AT-HOME PREPARATION

1. Choose a day to visit the shelter when you have plenty of time to look around. Try to go on a weekday, when shelters are quieter. Avoid Saturday or Sunday, if you can.

2. Arrange a time when as many family members as possible can come. If children are going to help choose the dog, be sure to explain that this process cannot be rushed and so you may not bring home a dog that day. You will avoid a bad experience for your entire family if you take your time.

3. Review your Dog File to remind yourself of your needs in regard to size, grooming, exercise, and personality. (Always keep your needs in mind. For example, if you have little time for grooming, you do not want a dog that needs daily brushing. If your exercise time is limited, you do not want a breed that requires a daily run. If you do not want to go through the growth stages of puppyhood, look only at adult dogs.)

4. If you live in a rented apartment, house, or condominium, let your landlord know of your plans to acquire a pet. Make sure he or she knows that you intend to be a responsible pet owner.

5. Take a tennis ball and a leash.

AT THE SHELTER

1. Walk through the kennels once and check out *all* the dogs.

2. When you see one that interests you, observe the dog's body language. Is it friendly when you speak to it? Does it appear confident and interested in you? Does it jump on the bars and bark or just wag its tail and try to communicate with you?

3. Talk to a shelter worker about the dog's history, age, breed mix, and shelter behavior. Check this information against the compatible breeds you have listed in your Dog File.

4. If the information fits your needs, ask for the dog to be removed from its enclosure. Now see how the dog relates to you in the open. Throw the tennis ball and see if it enjoys playing. Put the leash on its collar and see if it will walk with you. Give a "come" and a "sit" command and see if it has had obedience training. Pet it and notice how it accepts the body contact.

5. If you already own a dog, introduce it to the potential adoptee in the open area and allow them time to become acquainted.

6. If you decide that this is the dog for you, find out whether the shelter offers a trial period for evaluating the dog at home.

7. Take the dog to your veterinarian within three days for a health examination.

BRINGING THE DOG HOME

1. Arrange a time when you will have several days to get to know your dog and to help it adjust to its new environment.

2. Acquaint it with its feeding area, water bowl, sleeping quarters, and toys.

3. Remember that even a housebroken dog may make "mistakes" during the first few days as it adjusts to its new home. Be patient.

4. If you have children, explain to them that the dog needs to be handled gently, and that they should not disturb it when it is eating. Supervise them during the first few meals to make sure they understand.

5. Be clear about house rules. If you do not make them, your dog will. For instance, if you don't want your dog on the furniture, let both your dog and your family know this. Be consistent.

6. Make plans for your new dog's training program by either enrolling it in a class or setting up a home training schedule of your own.

7. If the dog has any physical or behavioral problems, call your veterinarian for advice.

Within one or two weeks, you should have a well-adjusted family member and a valuable friend. Your new orphan is a lucky dog to have found a home with an owner who is willing to prepare and care for it with responsibility and love.

CHAPTER 5

Choosing a Purebred

IF YOU ARE THINKING of acquiring a purebred
dog, there is no more enjoyable place to start your
search than a dog show. There is a magical feeling to the showgrounds. The
moment you enter the gates, you know that this territory belongs to dogs: dogs
whose ancestors have been bred to work, to hunt, to herd, and/or to offer
companionship to their owners. Within the confines of the arena, you can feast
your eyes on nearly every species of dog, from the tiny papillon with a pleasing
disposition and ears like butterfly wings to the thoughtful-looking basenji,
which yodels instead of barking; from the Rhodesian Ridgeback, a safari dog
with the shape of a dagger running down its back, to the rat-catching Bedlington terrier which looks like a lamb and the thick-coated Portuguese water dog,
which once carried fish between the boats of Portuguese fishermen.

WHAT TO EXPECT AT A DOG SHOW

From the formal competition grounds of Rottweil, Germany to friendly tree-
covered fairgrounds where families sit on the grass to watch their dogs compete
for blue ribbons or silver-plated serving dishes, dog shows are always popular
because they allow purebreds to "show their stuff." Certainly, very few of the
dogs actually win prizes. But dog-lovers never tire of the thrill of watching
dogs run gracefully across the breed ring, heel by the side of a pleased owner,
or jump over a wooden barrier and proudly bring back a wooden dumbbell.
Some winning dogs actually seem to grin . . . and why not? This is their opportunity to be acknowledged for their breeding and training.

The first dog show was held in 1859 in a town hall in Newcastle upon Tyne, England. Then, only hunting dogs were shown. Today the American Kennel club (AKC), which originated in 1884, registers over 120 breeds of dog. As you walk around the showgrounds, you will see different breeds and also a number of rings where females (bitches) and males (dogs) compete for conformation titles. Puppies are ring-eligible by six months and you will occasionally see dogs over ten years old competing. During this competition, a licensed AKC judge evaluates each dog according to the breed standard, by opening the mouth, looking at teeth, and observing the dog's structure and coat color. (Judges are licensed by the AKC after a trial period in which they learn to judge a certain breed. Not all judges can judge all breeds. Winning dogs are picked based on the breed standard, which is established by the breeders of that particular dog. The purpose of the show competition is to continue this "ideal" by conferring titles and thus encouraging the breeding of the best males and females.) After each dog is inspected, you will hear the judge say "Gait your dog." The dog will then be led, usually at a trot, across the ring by its handler. Many dogs have professional handlers who show the dog throughout its career. The judge watches the dog's gait and notes the physical coordination and balance that were not obvious when the dog was still. Finally, the judge selects a winner in each class and first- to fourth-place ribbons are presented. The last part of the ring competition is the "Best of Breed." The dogs entered in this competition are males and females that will be breeding. (At this point, if you are interested, you can talk to the owners about future litters.) Each ring competition lasts about one and one-half hours, so it is possible to observe a variety of breeds in one day.

THE GROUPS: THE DOG SHOW "WORLD SERIES"

If possible, arrange your day so you can stay for the late-afternoon event called "the groups." Into the group ring come the champions that were judged best of the breed on that day. They will now be judged against all of the other breeds in their class. The AKC divides dog breeds into seven groups. An announcer will inform you which group is showing and the name of the specific breed you are observing. This is the time to pull out your Dog File, take notes on your favorites, and watch the champions in action. Keep in mind that you will not necessarily see *every* type of dog in each group.

SPORTING DOGS

Sporting dogs originated in Europe; this energetic group is comprised of pointers, retrievers, setters, spaniels, vizslas, weimaraners, and wirehaired pointing griffons. They are placed in the sporting class because they were originally used for hunting, and in fact some still are today. Each of these "gun breeds" has its own aptitude and way of helping the hunter in sighting, pointing, setting, flushing, and retrieving game. Sporting dogs like being worked and they respond well to exercise and outdoor life.

HOUND DOGS

The twenty dogs which make up the hound group include some of the oldest breeds. Like the sporting dogs, they were bred to hunt, but unlike the "gun breeds," these dogs capture their prey using sight and scent. They can work in packs, and maintain a high degree of stamina and team spirit. These dogs follow directions well and view the master as the "pack leader." The twenty hound breeds are the Afghan, basenji, basset, beagle, black-and-tan coonhound, bloodhound, borzoi, dachshund, American and English foxhounds, greyhound, harrier, Ibizan, Irish wolfhound, Norwegian elkhound, otter hound, Rhodesian Ridgeback, saluki, Scottish deerhound, and whippet. Because of their origin and training, these hounds love exercise and do not tolerate a sedentary life. (The exception is the dachshund, which requires only minimal exercise.)

WORKING DOGS

The working dog group contains canines which are truly impressive in size and physical ability. The eighteen dogs in this group are Akita, Alaskan malamute, Bernese mountain dog, boxer, bullmastiff, Doberman pinscher, giant schnauzer, Great Dane, Great Pyrenees, komondor, kuvasz, mastiff, Newfoundland, Rottweiler, St. Bernard, Samoyed, Siberian husky, and standard schnauzer. Because of their dependability and intelligence, many of these dogs originally worked as guard dogs, using their natural instincts to defend their territory. Some of them still perform this work. Many others act courageously on their own initiative; indeed, the Newfoundland and St. Bernard, thought to be descended from the Tibetan mastiff, have proven reputations for saving lives.

TERRIERS

Terriers are known as the "earth dogs" because they hunt by digging and burrowing into the earth. Given this skill, many of the terriers are necessarily small to medium in build, but they make up for this lack of stature with large-sized determination! They were often used to hunt foxes that disappeared into the brush or to chase after badgers as they burrowed into the earth. Many of them are natural "ratters" and have earned a reputation for helping farmers exterminate vermin at harvest time. The twenty-three terriers recognized by the AKC are the Airedale, American Staffordshire, Australian, Bedlington, Border bull,

bull, cairn, Dandie Dinmont, fox, Irish, Kerry blue, Lakeland, Manchester, miniature schnauzer, Norfolk, Norwich, Scottish, Sealyham, Skye, soft-coated wheaten, Staffordshire bull, Welsh, and West Highland white. Terriers are playful, determined chasers, and have a serious bark that can alert you to intruders.

TOYS

When the toy group comes up, a change of pace is in the offing. A table is brought into the ring and each dog is placed on top of it so the judge can inspect and evaluate. The toy breeds, often referred to as the aristocrats of the ring, have never been working dogs. They are bred solely for the pleasure and comfort of their owners and their "work" is to give loving companionship. You will recognize a number of them as miniaturized versions of dogs in the other classes. The breeds are affenpinscher, Brussels griffon, Chihuahua, English toy spaniel, Italian greyhound, Japanese chin, Maltese, miniature pinscher, papillon, Pekingese, Pomeranian, pug, Shih Tzu, silky terrier, toy Manchester terrier, toy poodle, and Yorkshire terrier.

NON-SPORTING DOGS

Originally these dogs were used for hunting or working but now they no longer fit into either of those categories. Instead, they are bred as companion dogs. This group, which includes breeds from all over the world, contains an interesting and popular assortment of dogs: bichon frise, Boston terrier, bulldog, chow chow, Dalmatian, French bulldog, keeshond, Lhasa apso, poodle, schipperke, and Tibetan terrier.

HERDING DOGS

This group, which was originally included under the working dog classification, has a slighter build than the working class dogs; its members were used to herd sheep and to protect the herd from intruding wolves. Dogs in this group are the Australian cattle dog, bearded collie, Belgian Malinois, Belgian sheepdog, Belgian Tervuren, Bouvier des Flandres, briard, collie (rough- and smooth-coated), German shepherd, Old English sheepdog, puli, Shetland sheepdog, Welsh corgi (Cardigan), and Welsh corgi (Pembroke). (The sheepdog demonstration is especially fun. Sheepdogs are smart, calm, and capable of great speed. They can respond to as many as a dozen commands. If you get the opportunity to see this demonstration, try not to miss it. You will see the catlike movement of the dogs as they approach the flock and the hypnotic eye-control they use on the sheep.)

Once you have finished watching the groups and talking to the breeders, you should be familiar with several breeds that excite you. Be sure to take notes on these favorites and put them in your Dog File. You will be able to look up these breeds in the dog books and magazines that you have collected. At this point, you may also be tempted to start looking at puppies. Try to resist. There is one more step to take before you begin to evaluate puppies: You need to know the best place to purchase a purebred dog.

WHERE TO FIND THE BEST PUREBREDS

There are two types of breeders: good and bad. If you fall in love with a puppy from the wrong place, you may end up with an expensive and heartbreaking education in how *not* to choose a dog.

HOW MUCH IS THAT DOGGIE IN THE WINDOW?

The moment that the Moran family saw the three-month-old Dalmatian puppy peering eagerly out of its window in the pet shop at the mall, they knew they had to have it. They had been talking about getting a dog for several months, but had not planned on acquiring one that afternoon. The information card on the dog's cage told them that it was a new arrival from the Midwest and had been registered with the AKC. When they took the puppy out of its cage, it seemed a little withdrawn, but the store manager assured them that it would be playful once it was in a normal home environment. After five minutes in the arms of their nine-year-old son Tommy, the puppy "persuaded" them to take it home.

But Kelso just was not what the Morans had hoped for in a family pet. Even after he had adjusted to his new home, he sulked if no one was playing with him. At six months, he entered obedience school, had two fights with a weimaraner puppy, and almost flunked out. He obeyed the instructor in class but usually balked at commands from Tommy or Mrs. Moran. The obedience trainer felt that Kelso was overly insecure and asked the Morans about the pup's lineage. Mrs. Moran called the pet shop to inquire but was told that no information was available on him. Then, at ten months, Kelso developed another problem: He began snapping at Tommy's friends. When a snap turned into a bite, Kelso was given away.

What went wrong? Keep in mind that not every puppy purchased at a pet shop develops behavioral problems, but pet shop owners often are not as concerned as breeders with puppies' breeding and socialization. Living alone in a cage during the crucial socialization period (eight to sixteen weeks) is the worst possible beginning for a puppy's personality. As a result of this caged-in life, puppies often develop physical problems, such as "kennel cough" or other respiratory infections. In addition, if they remain in the pet shop too long they can develop "kennel syndrome," becoming withdrawn, depressed, and unsociable. And like children who are isolated early in life, these puppies can have emotional scars that turn into permanent behavioral problems.

To be sure, pet shop puppies often have AKC papers, but this is only an indication that the litter has been registered with the AKC. It tells nothing of the puppies' parents, health, or environment, and this information is generally not available when you buy puppies from stores. In addition, there are no litter siblings or mother dog to evaluate, no kennel to inspect, no breeder to offer advice and help with the puppy's future. In fact, because of these factors, national breed clubs forbid their members to sell litters to such pet businesses. So where do these puppies come from? Generally they come from "puppy mills," where dogs are bred without concern for health, disposition, or body structure. Shockingly, an estimated 500,000 puppies are "mass-produced" and sold to pet shops each year.

THE RIGHT SOURCES

The best place to purchase a purebred puppy is from a breeder who belongs to a local breed club. These breed clubs exist to promote the health and well-being of their dogs; members must abide by the organization's standards in order to belong. How can you find them? You may already have talked to a breed club member at the dog show; if so, you will have access to the club's location and meeting times. These clubs are valuable sources of information on health and training. Local obedience clubs are also a good source of information. They train a number of different breeds; pay a visit not only to see many different dogs with excellent training but also to inquire about reliable breeders in your area.

Another reliable source is the American Kennel Club, 51 Madison Avenue, New York, New York 10010; write and ask for a list of the breed specialty clubs in your area.

THE BREED DECISION

You have made the decision to acquire a dog. You've settled on a breed. You have decided that you want a puppy rather than an adult dog. You even have found a local breed club. Now your next step is to ask for a list of available puppy litters. Start visiting local breeders to see their dogs and get a sense of their approach to breeding. Keep a list of questions to ask each breeder, such as:

1. Does the breeder have genetic testing procedures? (If a breed has a health problem that is carried from one generation to the next, reliable breeders will test for this through X-ray and medical evaluations. After all, good health and temperament are as important to a good breeder as they are to you.)

2. Is there a health guarantee?

3. Can you have the puppy examined by your veterinarian?

4. If you can visit the sires of the litter, inquire if there were previous breedings from the same pair. (If so, you will have a chance to see the kind of puppies they produce. Many breeders say that puppies get their looks and disposition from their grandparents, so if you are lucky enough to meet any of them, it is an added bonus to your research.)

5. For each dog you see, ask about its temperament and observe its personality.

Thoughtful breeders will ask you about your home environment and your reasons for wanting a puppy, because they are interested in where their puppies will live and how they will be cared for.

When talking to breeders, use your Need Assessment to let them know what you are looking for in a puppy. (Keep a page in your file for each dog that interests you.) Remember that the breeders have watched these puppies since birth, so they know the merits of each puppy. If you find a breeder and a litter you like, fill in the information below and put it into your file.

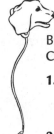

BREEDER ASSESSMENT FORM

Breeder:
Club Affiliation:

1. Observations on litter:
   Dam:
   Sire:

2. Information on individual puppies (have each puppy wear a different ribbon for easy identification):

3. Sibling relationships:

4. Background on parents and grandparents:
   Health:
   Disposition:
   Show and Obedience Competition:

5. Health Guarantee:

PUPPY TESTING

Once you have found the breeder that you like who has an available litter, how do you decide which puppy is best for you? Evaluating the litter with a temperament test is helpful. Puppy testing is one way to help you decide which puppy best matches your needs. The testing points will give you a feeling for the puppies' confidence, curiosity, ability to bond to a new person, reaction to being dominated, fears, retrieving instincts, scenting ability, and drive for leadership. The results will help you determine if a puppy is aggressive enough to be a guard dog or gentle enough to serve as a companion for the elderly.

One Sunday morning, I watched as a litter of nine seven-week-old Rottweiler puppies received their introduction into the human world. It was clear just from watching what kind of dog companions they would become. The prospective dog owners sat in a semicircle. In the house, the mother dog watched anxiously as, one by one, her pups were separated from her and their littermates and brought to the grassy area where we sat.

Twelve-year-old John sat eagerly with his parents. He knew that by the afternoon he would be bringing home a new friend. The man to my right already had an obedience-trained female Rottweiler and now wanted a male with *Schutzhund* potential. (See page 71 for a description of *Schutzhund* training.) The husband and wife to my left were getting their first Rottweiler. They wanted a watchdog, but one that would be easy to train. Another couple brought an elderly parent who wanted an easy going female for companionship and a sense of security. In less than two hours, three puppies were selected. Even though they came from the same litter, the puppies each had a unique temperament, and each went to an owner with unique needs.

THE PUPPY TEMPERAMENT TEST

The best time for puppy testing is during the puppies' seventh week; the optimum hour for the test is just before feeding time. Some breeders arrange for testing, so all you need to do is bring your Dog File and record the results. If evaluations are not part of the breeder's routine, you can do the testing yourself. Bring someone who is able to record the results for you. The puppy testing scores are one indication of how a dog will grow up and relate to its master. Information from the breeder adds to this profile. You may want to review your breed information from books and magazines before making your final selection. No matter how the puppy scores when tested, the training and environment you provide will influence what kind of dog it grows up to be. The items you'll need are: a crumpled-up ball of paper, a can with pennies in it, and a soft towel. The puppies can be evaluated indoors or out, but they *must* be away from their mother. Usually each puppy in the litter is identified by a different colored neck ribbon, making it easy for the scorekeepers and puppy buyers to record the correct results.

In your Dog File, on a sheet marked "Puppy Testing," indicate each puppy's collar color (or description, if it does not have a ribbon around its neck). Have each puppy brought to you in an area away from its den. You will evaluate the puppy for about five minutes. In order that the results be as accurate as possible, try to treat each puppy the same. Circle the number that best describes the puppy's behavior.

TEST 1: EVALUATING THE PUPPY'S SOCIAL ATTRACTION TO A PERSON AND ITS LEVEL OF CONFIDENCE IN A NEW SITUATION.
Have the puppy placed on the ground about five feet from you. Kneel down and gently clap your hands, coaxing the puppy to come to you. Don't call it.

Comes eagerly, tail up, jumps and bites at your hands	1
Comes readily, tail up, paws and licks your hands	2
Comes readily, tail down	3
Comes hesitantly, tail down	4
Does not come at all	5

TEST 2: MEASURING THE PUPPY'S DEGREE OF INDEPENDENCE AND ABILITY TO BOND TO YOU.
Stand up and walk away from the puppy but do not call it. Be sure the puppy sees you walking away.

Follows readily, tail up, gets underfoot, bites at feet	1
Follows readily, tail up, gets underfoot, no biting	2
Follows readily, tail down	3
Follows hesitantly, tail down	4
Does not follow or walks away	5

TEST 3: MEASURING THE PUPPY'S REACTION TO BEING DOMINATED.
Crouch down and gently roll the puppy onto its back and place your hand on its chest for a full thirty seconds.

Struggles fiercely, flails and tries to bite	1
Struggles fiercely, flails	2
Struggles, then relaxes	3
Does not struggle	4
Does not struggle, tries to avoid eye contact	5

TEST 4: MEASURING THE PUPPY'S REACTION TO SOCIAL DOMINANCE.
Kneel beside the puppy and let it stand while you stroke it from head to tail for thirty seconds.

Jumps, bites and growls	1
Jumps and paws at your hands	2
Squirms and licks at your hands	3
Rolls over and licks at your hands	4
Goes away and does not return	5

TEST 5: MEASURING THE PUPPY'S LEVEL OF CONFIDENCE AND ABILITY TO ACCEPT SOCIAL DOMINANCE.
Bend over and cradle the puppy under its belly, fingers interlaced, and hold it several feet off the ground for thirty seconds.

Struggles fiercely, bites and growls	1
Struggles fiercely, growls	2
Struggles, then relaxes	3
Struggles, relaxes and licks your hands	4
Does not struggle at all, may lick your hands	5

TEST 6: MEASURING THE PUPPY'S SENSITIVITY TO SOUND.
Shake the can of coins just a few feet from the puppy.

Walks toward can confidently and barks	1
Looks toward sound and barks	2
Investigates cautiously	3
Appears frightened, crouches and runs away	4
Cringes, backs off, hides	5

TEST 7: MEASURING THE PUPPY'S APTITUDE FOR RETRIEVING AND WILLINGNESS TO WORK.
Kneel down beside the puppy and attract its attention with a crumpled-up ball of paper. When the puppy takes notice, toss the ball five feet in front of its head.

Chases ball, picks it up and runs away	1
Chases ball, stands over it but does not return	2
Chases ball and returns it to you	3
Chases ball and returns to you without it	4
Starts to chase ball, loses interest	5

TEST 8: MEASURING THE PUPPY'S SENSITIVITY TO TOUCH.
Locate the webbing on one of the puppy's front feet and press it lightly between your finger and thumb, then more firmly until puppy responds. Count slowly from one to 10. Release as soon as the puppy pulls away or shows discomfort.

8 to 10 counts before release	1
6 to 7 counts	2
5 to 6 counts	3
2 to 4 counts	4
1 to 2 counts	5

TRANSLATING THE SCORE
Puppies that score two or more 1s might grow up to be extremely dominant, possibly aggressive. They may be quick to bite. Such a puppy would not be good with children or elderly people. In addition, if this dog has a 1 in touch sensitivity (Test 8), it could be difficult to train and probably would require a very experienced obedience trainer. This puppy has an aptitude for police dog work.

Puppies which score two or more 2s will tend to be dominant and most likely will need strong, consistent obedience training. This may require patience and someone who has plenty of time for training. However, once this dog learns to respect its leader, it can be a good working dog. This is an active, outgoing puppy which will work well with high-energy adults and teenagers. Again, this is not a good dog for homes with elderly people or small children.

Puppies which score two or more 3s accept human leadership easily. This dog will adapt well to new situations and is good with elderly persons and small children. Most likely, this is a stable dog with good potential for obedience training.

Puppies which score two or more 4s tend to be submissive and can adapt to most households. This dog will probably be less outgoing and active than the one scoring more 3s. It responds well to praise and encouragement in obedience training. This type of dog will do well with elderly owners and with young people, although children should be warned not to be rough with the dog during its puppyhood.

Puppies which score two or more 5s are extremely submissive and may need special handling to build up their confidence. Such a puppy would not be a good prospect for a first dog, because it does not adapt well to new situations and its behavior may therefore be unpredictable. If you are considering this puppy, have it retested in several days and recheck your Need Assessment to make sure this is what you want.

Choosing a Purebred Adult

You may decide on an adult purebred, and there are two good sources for you to consider. One is breeders who may have adult dogs that are well trained and no longer fit breeding stock requirements. These dogs have had an excellent home. In addition, you can see exactly what kind of dog you are getting. If you are interested in such a dog, contact the breed clubs and veterinarians in your community to get a list of breeders. The other source is purebred rescue groups. Rescued dogs are less expensive than those sold by the breeders. Many rescue organizations are sponsored by local breed clubs, who take rescued dogs into their homes until good owners are found. The dogs are usually spayed or neutered, so you will not be able to show or breed them. Purebred rescue groups know their breeds and are excellent sources of information on temperament and behavior.

CHAPTER **6**

Children and Dogs

Achild and a dog is a natural pairing. A dog can provide a child with pleasure, a catalyst for exercise, and security and protection. Dogs teach children to respect life and allow them to experience the giving and receiving of love. In addition, dogs can assist children in their growth and development. Children gain a sense of control and confidence when accompanied by a dog. If the correct dog is selected and integrated into the family, it will set the pattern for teaching children skills such as decision-making, sharing, and discipline and will help children maintain good mental health. But none of this happens by magic.

YOUR CHILD AND THE SELECTION PROCESS

Almost every child would like to have a dog, and caring for a canine can help to build responsibility. In fact, many parents with whom I discussed pet ownership expressed the hope that acquiring a dog would help to teach their children a sense of responsibility. If your Need Assessment indicates that your number one priority in acquiring a dog is to have a companion for your child, realize that it takes time and work from each member of the family to create a healthy relationship between child and dog.

Involve your child in acquiring the dog from day one. Your child can help to set up the Dog File or perform age-appropriate research on different types of dogs. Family discussions at each step teach your child patience and problem-solving skills. As your child observes dogs at various locations, have him or her work on the list and begin to match each dog with the family's needs. As a family, you can evaluate the different dogs' needs for grooming and exercise. Include each child in canine selection and in setting up the care and training program. The more the child is involved in the process and excitement of dog selection, the better his or her motivation will be for taking care of the new pet.

INTRODUCING A NEW BABY TO YOUR DOG

Judy and Paul Howell were expecting their first child and wanted their two-year-old puli, Hobarth, to accept the new arrival. Because their dog had heretofore received all the attention, the Howells worried about jealousy or anger, so they planned the introduction between infant and canine very carefully. But it turned out not to be careful enough: The day Judy returned home from the hospital, Paul had brought lunch in so she wouldn't have to cook. They took a few minutes to introduce Hobarth to baby Naomi, then returned the infant to her crib. Almost immediately, the baby started crying. Judy and Paul hurried into the nursery, closing the door behind them; Hobarth was not allowed into the nursery. That was too much for the dog. He walked into the kitchen and demolished the lunch. When Paul came out of the nursery, he saw the last of the lunch being devoured and yelled at the dog. That evening, Hobarth "forgot" his housetraining for the first time since he was a puppy and eliminated on the rug. The Howells realized that Hobarth was in the throes of "sibling rivalry" and acted quickly to give him love and attention and include him in the family's activities.

Parents must realize that jealousy or sibling rivalry is not limited to children; Hobarth, like an older brother or sister, needed to be prepared in advance for the baby. Like all dogs, he was curious, and because he had never been exposed to babies, he did not know how to react to the new member of the family. Most dogs perceive babies as part of their family and will respond to them as they would to a sibling puppy—with interest and protection. But in order to make this happen smoothly, the dog needs to be prepared properly so that the relationship can develop into a nurturing friendship.

BEFORE THE BABY ARRIVES

1. Several months before delivery, refresh your dog's obedience training. This will make it easier to put your dog on a "stay" command and to correct any jumping up when the baby is being held.

2. Because dogs learn to accept someone new by smelling and hearing, introduce your dog to other infants while you're still pregnant. If

possible, and under supervision, let it get used to the way a baby smells. Let your dog hear a baby crying; it needs to know that a crying baby is a normal part of family life.

3. Expose the dog to different types of baby items that you will be using, such as noisemakers, toys, clothes, and so on.

4. Bring your pet into the nursery and let it get used to the room, including smells and furniture placement. (You might even want to bring home a dirty diaper before the baby arrives, to introduce the dog to the newborn's scent.)

5. Stock up on dog toys and treats so your dog will have something new to engage it while you are with the baby.

WHEN THE BABY COMES HOME

1. The mother should let the father carry the child into the house so she can greet the dog without holding the baby. The dog will not have to restrain its enthusiastic welcome and the mother will not be distracted. This also prevents the mother's first greeting to the dog from being a reprimand about jumping up.

2. Introduce your dog to the baby as soon as possible. Put your dog in a sit/stay command and bring the baby into the room. If the dog remains calm and under control, you can let it approach the baby. Be sure that someone in the family is in charge of the dog while someone else holds the baby.

3. Give your dog plenty of treats and toys. Your dog will begin to associate the baby's presence with positive reinforcement.

4. Avoid allowing the dog under the crib or cradle. Dogs can upset a crib or cradle or knock down the side rails. As a general rule, the baby's toys and equipment should be off-limits to the dog. Give a clear "no" whenever its interest in these items is aroused, and find something else for the dog to play with.

5. Be present whenever the dog and baby are together. Your presence will remind the dog that you are in charge and ensure a calm interaction between the two new friends—as well as giving you peace of mind.

6. Set a time each day when you can play with your dog alone. This way, your canine will know that a new family member does not mean rejection.

7. Be patient with your dog. Some animals revert to "childhood" and need to be housetrained again. This will pass with retraining and patience.

When you have planned this occasion carefully, you will find that your dog and baby will be able to begin a healthy relationship; indeed, your dog will be happy to have someone to play with and protect.

DOGS AND PRESCHOOLERS

As children begin to explore and learn about their ever-expanding world, a dog's presence can help. Encouraging your toddler to play with an accepting, loving dog will widen the child's scope. For example, dogs serve as useful models for the toddler in forming positive relationships. By touching and talking to the family dog, a baby develops the feelings of warmth, security, and love which are critical in these years. Dogs also serve as incentive for movement. Often a baby will follow a dog's movement with its eyes and then try the same movement. A dog is particularly helpful during the child's crawling stage and later when the child learns to walk. Oftentimes a child's first word is the name of his or her dog.

When Randy was two, his old English sheepdog, Harry, helped him improve his verbal skills. Randy liked to "talk" to his dog during breakfast. Naturally, Harry "talked" back. Randy learned his first word, "woof," after listening to the dog bark. Randy also used the dog to develop his tactile sense; as an infant, he would lie beside the dog and cuddle with it until both were contentedly asleep. When he was ready to walk, he would gently grab onto the dog's coat and pull himself up. Then the two of them would carefully step around the house.

Interaction with a dog is also an excellent way for toddlers to learn socialization concepts, such as gentleness and respect for others. Using the dog as a model, you can explain that living things need to be respected. Begin by telling the child not to do anything to the dog that might hurt it. (For instance, in picking up a puppy, it is important that children support the puppy with one hand under the chest and the other under the rear of the belly. Picking up a puppy by the scruff of the neck is not good for it.) Setting guidelines for your child's treatment of the family dog will give your toddler a sense of security. (By the time your child is two, he or she may want to test the rules; simply remind him or her of the dog's limits. This gives your child a tangible example of guidelines.) A dog can also have a wonderful effect on a youngster's self-esteem. (Toddlers can sit on the floor and be at eye level with their dog. This experience helps the youngster feel worthwhile and helps to build a positive self-image.)

The feelings of love and security that toddlers receive from their mothers are sometimes transferred back to pets. A youngster often treats a pet the same way he or she is treated. If you listen in on a conversation, you will hear the child imitating the parents as he or she talks to the dog; the child will say, "Good puppy," or "Bad dog." Since a dog helps a child feel loved and safe, it is a good choice as a pet. Promoting a link between the child and the dog will help your toddler recognize his or her individuality as he or she works out feelings toward others. In addition, your child will find the family dog to be a protector and an enthusiastic and playful friend.

DOGS AND OLDER CHILDREN: TEACHING RESPONSIBILITY

In many cases, dealing with a new dog is the first opportunity for a child to have a "parenting" experience and to think beyond his or her own needs and wishes. Children depend on their parents for love, care, and attention; with the acquisition of a new canine, they can put into practice what they have learned. A child can protect, feed, exercise, play with, and offer love to a dog; the bonus is that the dog will almost always respond with affection and attention. And as children help in training the dog, they learn that being a "parent" means setting limits and saying no.

GUIDELINES FOR TEACHING RESPONSIBILITY

Carrie, age eleven, wanted a dog very much. She pleaded with her parents almost every day. But her parents, Bruce and Judy, were reluctant because Carrie had shown signs of irresponsibility. For example, she never cleaned up her bedroom, did her homework only when it was demanded of her, and did not always complete her household chores satisfactorily. After discussing the matter, Bruce and Judy decided that acquiring a dog for Carrie—and putting her in complete charge of its care—might actually be a good move. They decided to adopt a dog from the local shelter. Carrie selected the dog she wanted and named him Homer. At first, she took on the dog's care with enthusiasm. After a few weeks, however, Carrie lost interest in Homer and stopped paying attention to him. The dog gradually lost his training and seemed listless. Bruce and Judy explained to Carrie about the change in the dog's behavior and how this was directly related to her lack of responsibility regarding the dog's care. Carrie did a complete turnaround: She not only took excellent care of Homer after that, but her other responsibilities—cleaning up her bedroom, doing her homework, performing household chores—were improved upon. Carrie finally understood the importance of responsibility.

The basic guidelines listed below will help you teach responsibility to your child through caring for a pet.

1. Involve your child in the selection of age-appropriate care jobs which he or she would like to be responsible for. (Ensuring age-appropriate tasks will give your child the optimal opportunity to succeed.)

2. Be sure that your child knows when to perform the chore and when it should be completed.

3. Praise your child when he or she fulfills the responsibility. This is important to your child's developing a sense of pride in his or her work.

4. Set up an evaluation period for you and your child. Be prepared to make amendments if, say, the dog care duties are too difficult or the time schedule is inconvenient.

5. Do not perform your child's duties. If your child gradually loses interest in his or her tasks, think up ways to keep the chores interesting, or reward your child every month or so for a job well done.

Below is a sample of a "Petition for Dog Ownership" which is something you may wish to institute with your child when acquisition of a pet is imminent. This contract stipulates the rules and regulations of dog ownership and the responsibilities you will expect your child to take on when the dog enters the home.

Petition for Dog Ownership

I, _____, request that a dog/puppy become a member of our family. I request that I be part of the selection process, that I be able to suggest its name, and that I be allowed to help take care of this pet. I would be willing to feed the dog on _____(day)_____, at _____(time)_____. I promise to exercise our dog daily by taking it outside to play and by taking it for walks. I would like to help with grooming by brushing and bathing it. When possible, I would like to accompany it to the veterinarian. When my friends are present, I will explain the house rules concerning the dog. I will watch doors and gates so it cannot leave the yard. I request that I take part in the obedience training. I will need help from others in the family for the following duties:

1.
2.
3.

I have talked to these family members (list names) and they have agreed to help in the areas mentioned.

This contract is to be reviewed weekly for one month and at the end of the month it may be rewritten after a family discussion. If this contract is not fulfilled, it will be brought to family conference for discussion and action.

Petitioner's Signature _____

Family Member's Approval _____

Date _____

If difficulties arise over the dog's care, a family conference is in order. Of course, the responsibilities as originally set should be taken seriously, but flexibility is needed if a child's grades or social schedule begin to cause conflict. Although having a dog helps to build character and responsibility in children, the main reason to have a family dog is to bring additional joy to the family, so try not to look at dog care as drudgery.

DOG TRAINING AND CHILDREN

Dogs that are most appropriate for children are those which adapt well to family life and are reliable, affectionate, outgoing, playful, and easy to train. However, keep in mind that no matter how much research you do, or how many breeders or shelters you talk to, the dog's behavior is dependent on training. Involving your youngster in the dog's training is good for both the dog and the child. (Off-leash puppy training is the first step in teaching your child to train your dog. If you adopt an adult dog, your child should take part in the obedience classes.) Because each dog is an individual with a distinct personality, dog training teaches children problem-solving skills by trial and error.

Training a dog requires the child to concentrate, make good eye contact, and give direct messages. This activity carries over to the youngster's learning patterns: A child not only goes to obedience school with the dog but he or she learns that "homework" is a must. No dog learns without consistent home practice. Puppies need frequent praise and clear limits as they learn. So do children. Working with a puppy which makes mistakes teaches a child that perseverance when things get tough can bring success. This is a step-by-step rehearsal for the educational ladder your child will someday climb. Also, puppy raising and dog training help children develop empathy for all forms of life and sound family values. The dog becomes well behaved and the child develops confidence and patience.

A child gets a feeling of self-worth by teaching his or her dog and by watching the dog obey. As the child praises the dog for good behavior, he or she begins to develop a personal standard of behavior. In addition, a child will feel less anxious about parents' limit-setting when he or she acts as "parent" to a growing pup.

Dogs end up in animal shelters because their families give up on them. When children see their dog discarded in this way, they learn that loyalty and patience are not important values. (This experience is not easily forgotten as the child faces other challenges of growing up.) Fortunately, this negative lesson can be avoided with careful selection and responsible dog training.

INVOLVEMENT TRAINING PROGRAMS
FOR CHILDREN

The puppy raising program for Canine Companions for Independence (described in Chapter 12) gives youngsters the opportunity to bring up a puppy that will offer a service to the physically handicapped. National 4-H clubs offer dog care and training projects in which youngsters learn handling and obedience training. They also have a puppy raising project where children socialize a puppy candidate for guiding the blind. (The children receive a two-month-old puppy, give it love and basic obedience work and, at the end of one year, give the puppy to a guide dog school.) Information on 4-H programs is available by writing to the National 4-H Council, 7100 Connecticut Avenue, Washington, D.C. 20015.

Another activity that teaches children a lesson in values is a part of dog training called showmanship. In Junior Showmanship, boys and girls between the ages of ten and seventeen receive awards and trophies for their dog handling skills. Dogs must be registered with the American Kennel Club and competition takes place at local dog shows. The Junior Showmanship clubs are sponsored by local dog clubs and information on this activity is available by writing to the American Kennel Club, 51 Madison Avenue, New York, New York 10010.

THE BENEFITS TO YOUR CHILD OF KEEPING
A HEALTHY DOG

Maintaining a dog's health is not only essential for the dog's well-being but educational for your child. During the puppy's early examinations, the youngster can form a relationship with the dog's doctor and learn the meaning of preventive health care. This introduction to animal medicine allows the child to become an ongoing partner in his or her puppy's health program. Younger children can overcome some of their own fears about vaccinations as they reassure their puppy about getting a shot. Many veterinarians will encourage the child to observe the puppy's health exam and to learn what to be alert for regarding common canine ailments. Your child's trusting relationship with the vet will most likely extend to the pet's physical well-being and will give your child another boost in responsibility and maturation.

LEARNING ABOUT BIRTH AND DEATH

Another benefit of dog ownership is the knowledge children acquire about nature. Oftentimes a child has no understanding of birth; having an expectant dog can put the process into perspective. Indeed, watching the body change and being present at the birthing is a healthy way for small children to learn about this part of nature. When the decision to spay the female dog is made, an explanation about unwanted puppies offers another lesson.

Children deal with the loss of their pets in different ways, depending on age and experience with separation. A toddler might not miss his playmate, but the school-age child will want to have an explanation for the dog's disappearance. Most older children respond to the death of a dog with the same stages of grief that adults experience: denial, sadness, anger, and finally, letting go. They may exhibit symptoms such as nightmares, insomnia, anger toward parents (and maybe veterinarians), or guilt. Parents can help their children by encouraging them to express their sorrow and by trying to empathize with them. The following activities can help your child deal with the loss of a pet.

1. Encourage your child to put his or her feelings into words; this may be hard, but it is important for your child to purge the hurtful feelings before they become too deeply rooted. Talk about the enjoyable experiences your child shared with the dog. This helps your child say good-bye and gives him or her a more realistic way to deal with the loss.

2. Encourage your child to draw a picture of the dog or make a scrapbook using photos of the animal.

3. Have your child write a poem or story about the dog. This is a constructive, creative outlet for grief that helps with the emotional healing.

When the child is ready (the waiting period is different for each child), a new pet can be brought in to fill the gap. One child may want the same breed, but a different color; another may want to switch to a different pet altogether. In any event, don't push your child into making a hasty decision.

There are two excellent books for parents to read on children losing pets; they are *Pet Loss* by Herbert Nieburg and Arlene Fischer (New York: Harper and Row, 1982) and *Coping with Sorrow on the Loss of your Pet* by Moira Anderson (Los Angeles: Peregrine Press, 1987). A good book for your child to read in order to understand pet loss is *The Tenth Best Thing About Barney* by Judith Viorst (New York: Atheneum, 1971).

Concepts such as birth and death are difficult for children to grasp. But learning about these two facets of nature through the family dog gives your child a foundation in reality and a way of discussing his or her feelings with the family.

CHILDREN AND UNFAMILIAR DOGS

Not all dogs are dependable with small children. Some dogs snap, and children are the most common bite victims. Dogs should be socialized and taught to be gentle with children, just as children should be taught to be considerate of dogs. Dogs should not be allowed to roam loose or wander unsupervised.

Children can unintentionally provoke dog bites. A dog which is awakened suddenly may be startled and attack. Also, youngsters may get excited and run toward a dog, not realizing that some dogs will react in a negative way. Teasing a dog with food or a toy can provoke a snarl, a snap, or even a bite. Some dogs may believe they are protecting your territory. Some may actually be frightened by a sudden intrusion into their yard.

What can parents teach a child so this negative experience can be avoided? Try always to accompany your child when he or she is confronting a strange dog. Until youngsters have the experience and the proper judgment to approach unfamiliar dogs, here are some guidelines that will help your child avoid difficult situations:

1. Never approach a strange dog. It is particularly important not to approach a dog which is fenced and protecting its yard.

2. Do not try to stop two dogs from fighting, even if one is the family dog.

3. Never approach a strange dog while it is eating or sleeping.

4. Do not feed or tease a strange dog.

If your child cannot avoid facing a strange dog, make sure he or she follows these rules:

1. Stand quietly with your arms at your sides.

2. Do not shout at the dog.

3. Do not wave your arms or grab at the dog. Do not make any sudden movements.

4. Do not run away. Some dogs may think the child is prey and chase the youngster.

5. If a dog looks frightened or angry, growls or bares its teeth, be especially careful not to move toward it in any way.

6. If a dog approaches and looks upset, do not stare directly into its eyes. Some dogs interpret this as a challenge.

Very few dogs bite. However, anticipating and guarding against potential problems can prevent an unpleasant experience that could affect a child's relationship with his or her own dog.

CHAPTER 7

Educating Your Dog

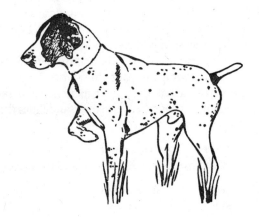

Your dog's education must begin at once, not after bad habits have been acquired. It is always easier to learn a new skill than to unlearn a bad habit. A case in point: When the Rubins selected their four-month-old puppy, Watson, they made two major errors. They purchased him without learning about his litter history or socialization, and they did not begin a training program. By the time Watson was a year old, he had bitten a neighbor's child, eaten a hole in the living room rug, stolen food regularly from the kitchen counter, and torn up the rose garden. Mr. Rubin could usually get Watson to mind him, but the dog refused to obey his mistress.

Before you even meet your puppy, its developmental process is well under way. A puppy's first teachers are its mother and littermates. The early developmental stages vary according to breed and individual puppy, but there are distinct ages when you can expect to see certain changes. Puppyhood is divided into four stages: neonatal, transitional, socialization, and juvenile.

THE NEONATAL PERIOD: BIRTH TO TWO WEEKS

The newborn puppy is born deaf and blind; its first experience is feeling its mother's tongue licking off the watery sac which it has lived in for the past nine weeks. The puppy responds to this enthusiastic massage by starting to breathe and making its initial "mewing" sound. It instinctively begins to move its head from side to side in a "rooting" motion. When it locates the soft, warm body of its mother, it squirms up and down, seeking its first taste of milk. The puppy is born with a strong suckling instinct. However, it must learn that when it opens its mouth, its tongue will enclose the mother's nipple and, with vigorous movement of its neck and shoulders, along with kneading forepaws against the breast, it will get warm milk. The puppy seeks warmth and usually sleeps amid a bundle of littermates in order to maintain a comfortable body temperature. During this two-week period, the puppy's brain has not developed sufficiently for it to eliminate on its own, so the mother helps her charge by licking the anal and genital glands of the puppy, stimulating elimination and keeping the puppy and nest clean. Most of the puppy's first two weeks of life is spent sleeping; it usually wakes only to eat and to receive a cleaning from its mother.

THE TRANSITIONAL PERIOD: TWO WEEKS TO THREE WEEKS

Despite breed and individual differences, most puppies open their eyes at about fourteen days and can respond to sound by twenty-one days. With new senses and developing muscles, they not only react to sound but can crawl backwards and even attempt an unsteady walk. Although the mother continues to clean the babies, they move away from the nest and eliminate on their own. They engage playfully with littermates by pawing and biting. Tailwagging and licking are puppies' first response to human contact.

According to Dr. Ian Dunbar, an animal behaviorist and author of *Dog Behavior: Why Dogs Do What They Do* (Neptune, N.J.: T.F.H. Publications, Inc., 1979), it is possible to train fifteen-day-old puppies to respond to certain cues in exchange for a food reward. He states that three-week-old puppies develop the ability to recognize a painful experience and can learn to avoid it. The puppy continues to seek out warm, comfortable places and it will avoid cold surfaces and unpleasant smells. At this age, the seed for future housetraining is evident.

THE SOCIALIZATION PERIOD: THREE WEEKS TO TWELVE WEEKS

During this period, the puppy's experience with its environment forms its personality. Veterinarian Michael Fox, an animal behaviorist who is director of the Institute of Animal Problems of the Humane Society of the United States, has done extensive research with both dogs and wolves. He describes in his book, *Understanding Your Dog* (New York: Bantam, 1981), how at three and a half to four weeks, puppies begin to interact with each other by chewing ears, pawing, and licking each other's faces. He believes that the puppies learn from this play process to inhibit their bites and to gauge how much pain they are allowed to inflict on each other. Puppies which are taken away from the litter before this time may not learn how hard they can "play" with their future human family.

According to Dr. Fox, the period from four to five weeks is when the puppies begin to learn their defensive-protective pattern by guarding favorite tug-of-war objects or pieces of food from one another. Both physical and social skills are developed and set patterns for relationships with others.

At this time, puppies become great investigators, usually full of confidence and eager to learn. At about five weeks, the mother starts to wean her puppies; her snap or growl teaches another lesson: "No." This canine method of discipline lays the foundation for obedience training, when the new owner will need to discourage undesirable behavior with a firm, low-toned "no." Limits and discipline are completely natural to the beginning of puppy education.

Clarence Pfaffenberger, who began his research with the Guide Dogs for the Blind in 1946 while studying puppy breeding and training, has made great contributions to knowledge about dog behavior and learning. He describes puppies during their socialization period and how their early experiences with people contribute to their success as guide dogs. He reported in *The New Knowledge of Dog Behavior* (New York: Howell, 1981) that the period between twenty-one and twenty-eight days is crucial in behavior development because whatever the puppy learns at this time becomes fixed and influences its attitude toward man and animals throughout its life. Pfaffenberger found that if guide dog candidates did not receive the needed contact with people during these weeks, they were not able to learn appropriate tasks for the guide dog work.

For the puppy owner, then, the message is clear: The experiences that a puppy has with people during weeks three through twelve have a far greater impact than similar experiences in later months. The human-animal bond has been formed and the puppy is easier to teach during this critical time. Puppies that are raised in homes with ample human contact, especially with children, have a better opportunity of becoming good "family dogs" than those brought up in a kennel or in pet shop cages.

The best time to remove a puppy from its litter is between six and eight weeks. By then, both mother and littermates have made their imprint on the puppy and it has learned social rules. Now the puppy is ready to take its proper role in the family hierarchy and abide by the needs of the human pack.

THE JUVENILE PERIOD: TWELVE WEEKS TO SEXUAL MATURITY

The puppy during the juvenile period is similar to a human adolescent in that it experiences wide swings between the desire to explore independently and the desire to stay close to the home base. Michael Fox's research indicates that a vulnerable "fear period" develops at four to five months, when the puppy is extremely sensitive to trauma. Even though its attention span is brief, formal puppy training should begin by three months.

During this time, teething can be stressful to both puppy and owners; it helps to be prepared with an ample supply of rawhide bones. Puppies are also constantly testing the limits of permissible behavior at this time. Despite this rebellious learning pattern, they need the reassurance of firm leadership.

TEACHING YOUR PUPPY

When raising a child, parents do not wait for school to begin before they work to instill a love of learning in their child. Puppy training should be viewed with the same attitude. By understanding the stages of growth, you can motivate your puppy to respond to the rules of the house and to build a repertoire of skills and proper behavior. You may have selected the cream-of-the-crop puppy, but if you ignore its education it will never develop into that perfect dog you had hoped for.

Your puppy needs leadership from its "family pack" in order to gain a sense of security. Without it, you may have a problem dog which makes its own rules both at home and in your community. For example, the first night my puppy Lorelei came home, I almost let her sleep on my bed because I believed she was lonely and needed comfort. That would have been a horrible mistake. Luckily, I had read that whatever the dog learns as a puppy will last a lifetime: Having an eighty-five-pound adult Rottweiler sleeping on the bed at her whim was not what I needed.

Communicating with your dog and shaping its behavior are an essential part of your relationship. Training your dog to behave properly requires lots of love and respect. Dogs see and hear messages the moment they come into your home; they learn from your tone of voice, your body language, and your facial expressions.

Like children, puppies learn to imitate behavior. In fact, one of the easier ways to start your puppy off on the right paw is to let an older dog teach the younger one. Lorelei was four when I got my puppy Delilah. Lorelei quickly taught her new playmate everything she knew. She showed her where to eliminate outside, how to walk down the steep driveway in the morning to retrieve the paper, and the location of the best digging spots in the yard. Having an older dog is a great advantage for the new puppy owner, but be sure that the habits the older dog teaches are ones that you want taught!

TEACHING CAN BE FUN!

Elementary school teachers often have "Reading is Fun" signs in their classrooms. Educators know that this message encourages young children to like their introduction to reading; psychologists know that students learn more easily when they enjoy the task. Puppies are much the same. Utilizing the dog's natural instincts for fun—to explore and play—is the first rule of successful puppy training.

Puppies and dogs like approval. It is important to remember that when your dog does the right thing, lavish praise in an enthusiastic tone of voice should follow. My oldest Rottweiler is seven, but I still praise her with an enthusiastic "Good girl, Lorelei," when she does what she was trained to do. In addition, dogs tune in to the nonverbal messages we convey. It is sometimes easier to put energy into disapproval when a puppy does something wrong, but remember that attention paid to good behavior always pays off.

DEVELOPING YOUR LEADERSHIP

You can train your dog with confidence and leadership, but it requires practice and dedication. If you are consistent, fair, and patient, your dog will sense your authority and strength. Your puppy learned to follow its mother's authority and you, the new pack leader, are starting where the mother left off. Since you feed, exercise, play with, and direct your dog, it is natural that you move into the mother's place. If you watch a litter, you will see how clearly the mother makes her wishes known. A growl, a shake, or a disapproving look all give a clear message.

Working on your leadership training will make it easier to train your dog well. Here are a few suggestions that will improve your communication with your puppy:

1. Praise is the key to educating your dog. Every time your dog does something you approve of, respond with pleasure. Your words, your body, and your voice should all communicate what an amazingly wonderful puppy you are so lucky to have. Dogs can hear your approval and this reinforces their desire to please you.

2. Keep your tone of voice and your facial expressions consistent when you tell your puppy what you want. If you smile when you say "no" to a specific behavior, your rules will not be obeyed.

3. Make sure your puppy knows what the right behavior is before it receives any correction. The alternative to a disapproved action should be clear first.

4. Play with your puppy each day as you teach new behavior. Your puppy should learn that it is fun to obey you. If you both enjoy the time you spend together, a mutual bond will develop and will set the pattern for a long, rewarding relationship.

TRAINING YOUR DOG TO BECOME A GOOD FAMILY MEMBER

There is a period (between seven weeks and three months) when puppy training is entirely in your hands. Not only are you paving the way for the puppy's entrance into "nursery school," but you begin the process of housetraining. As the pack leader, you are responsible for teaching the rules of the house. This will include the dog's coming when called, eliminating outside in the area you choose, chewing only appropriate objects, learning not to bite, and allowing examination by you or a veterinarian. Teaching and directing your puppy's behavior is easier when you use its natural instincts. Both animals and humans are creatures of habit; it is always harder to change behavior once it is established.

LEARNING TO COME

One of the first things a puppy learns is to come when you call it by name. Psychology learning theory has taught us that animals learn by association, reward, and repetition. If your puppy associates pleasure with your call, it will want to come to you. Play with your puppy, bend down to its level, and let your voice be enthusiastic when you call. When it is playing and suddenly decides to come to you, take advantage of the action you are trying to teach by saying its name and the word, "come." Praise it for being so smart that it knows its name and the "come" command. Combining meals with learning "come" is effective and you always have your dog's attention. Have a dog treat in your pocket whenever you play, and treat your dog when it comes to your call. Never correct or punish your puppy when it comes to you. Your dog should associate pleasure and approval with your call. Repeat this activity several times a day and notice how quickly your puppy learns to come.

HOUSETRAINING: WHERE'S THE BATHROOM?

Teaching your puppy to go outside is one of the challenges of dog ownership. Teaching this behavior is a chance for you to make your leadership work. This training should be a positive one for both you and your puppy. Remember that when the puppy was between three and four weeks old, it began to move away from its den to eliminate. Keeping a den clean is a natural instinct for dogs. Making your new puppy a den/crate is the easiest and most efficient way of housetraining it. If the puppy does not have the opportunity to wander around the house and learn that it can eliminate on the rug, the pattern never gets started. With a wire, see-through crate, a puppy has a secluded, private den of its own and will refrain from eliminating in it. Your responsibility will be to anticipate when your puppy needs to go out. These times might include first thing in the morning, after naps, and right after mealtime.

Remember that your aim is to avoid "mistakes" in the house and to prevent such behavior from becoming a pattern. Decide in advance what area outside will be the dog's "bathroom" and take your puppy to the same place each time. Wait with your puppy, don't just leave it. After it has finished, praise it with an enthusiastic "good dog." You can also reward the behavior with a treat or with some outdoor play. (This need not be done every time the dog eliminates, but be sure your puppy knows you approve.) Puppies sleep a lot while they are growing, so the privacy of a comfortable den is ideal. If you work and the puppy is alone for some hours, you may have to put paper in a corner of the den. Be sure to remove papers when they are soiled so the puppy learns to be clean. Despite all this planning, some mistakes are going to be made in the house; the puppy will not be living twenty-four hours a day in the den. So if you catch the puppy in the act, shout at it and rush it outside. Never punish your puppy after the fact: This reaction will not change the unwanted behavior and the puppy could learn to become afraid of you. Praise your dog when it performs correctly; ignore it when it doesn't. The puppy quickly will learn that it gets attention for doing what you want. Success will motivate both you and your puppy for the next training experience.

NURSERY SCHOOL FOR PUPPIES

As soon as your puppy has had its last DHL (distemper, hepatitis, and lepto-spirosis) shot, at about three months old, it is ready to start puppy training classes. These may be held indoors, where you have more control, or outdoors, where the natural environment is more challenging but is more like your pup-py's backyard. Usually, the training is done in weekly classes and should be practiced at home, both on- and off-leash. Learning at this age utilizes the puppy's natural desire to play and channels this instinct into controlled behav-ior. Your dog is taught the basics, such as "come," "sit," and "down." When these exercises are performed correctly, your dog should be rewarded with en-thusiastic praise and treats. The puppy also is taught to run on your left side (heeling), on- and off-leash. The desire to stay with you depends on the per-sonality of the puppy. Some are easily distracted and require more patience.

OFF-LEASH PUPPY TRAINING

Play training is an education for the master as well as the puppy. They *both* learn how to follow the required exercises. One Sunday morning in the park, I watched as six playful puppies and their eager owners began a play training class taught by Vicky Arnold of Companion Dog Training in Los Angeles. Arnold was trained by Dr. Ian Dunbar, a Berkeley animal behaviorist who de-veloped a method called Sirius puppy training in 1982. His socialization train-ing for puppies starts when they are three to four months old. Weekly sessions mold a solid temperament in the puppy by the age of six months. Puppies are rewarded with treats, praise, and play.

Most obedience training is taught by using leash corrections; the dogs wear loose chain collars, and the owners jerk on the leash to get their dogs' attention. This method can discourage both owner and dog when the correc-tion is applied improperly. In Dr. Dunbar's sessions, all the classes are off-leash and the training is integrated into activities that a dog enjoys. The entire family is encouraged to join the sessions; even children take an active part in teaching the puppies to be tolerant of handling and eating interruptions. The children hand-feed the puppies and the dogs learn to associate strange children with food treats. Since most dog bites occur with youngsters, this is a valuable lesson for a young puppy to learn.

In the session I observed, the puppies started off in a free-for-all play session where they chased and jumped on each other. We watched as Jenna, a four-month-old Labrador retriever, chased Sasha, a puli mix, under the bench. Sasha's owner moved over apprehensively to lend her dog support, but Vicky Arnold stopped her.

"Don't pet Sasha when she hides, it will reinforce her nervousness," Arnold said.

Sasha recovered and went after Rudi, a Lhasa apso which had come with two teenage owners. After five minutes of play, Arnold brought the group together for their first exercise.

"Call your puppy's name, praise it when it stops playing and looks up at you. Then, when it comes, reward it with a liver treat," Arnold said.

Two puppies came eagerly. Rudi was having too much fun with Jenna, so he ignored the command.

"Rudi, COME!" called his owner, a mild-mannered lady who was fast losing her patience. The dog came and she said, "Good boy. Now, go play."

Along with the treat, each puppy got the additional reward of returning to play. This taught them that coming when called does not stop their fun time. After a few practices of "come" and "sit," each owner sat with his puppy for the body exam.

"Look at ears and teeth," Arnold said. "Be sure your dog gets used to your opening his mouth. Encourage kids to handle the dogs so the dogs will get used to rough-and-tumble games with them. Put your hands in their mouth every day. In a few months, these puppies will have adult jaws, so let's practice now."

Jenna struggled during the body exam but she wasn't allowed to go free until she relaxed.

This off-leash puppy training builds good temperament and gives the dog's family an enjoyable learning experience. When the course is over, the puppy is prepared to enjoy further obedience training.

OBEDIENCE TRAINING

Once a puppy has finished basic training, many dog owners want to continue to work with their dogs in improving their manners and temperament. Working with your dog regularly builds its confidence and gives you a measure of control over its behavior. Most dogs enjoy ongoing training if it is associated with play and praise

Dog obedience training is founded on the classic studies of conditioning and learning. The dog's behavior is shaped by a system of reward and punishment. It is conditioned to obey its owner by getting either enthusiastic praise or a jerk of the collar and a strong "no." As the process continues, the dog owner, too, is conditioned to a pattern of behavior. The owner learns to focus on the dog and to give clear, firm commands. The owner is rewarded for his or her efforts with an obedient dog. Both owner and pet are conditioned: the dog learns to behave and the owner learns a sense of his or her own power and authority.

Obedience classes are available in almost every community and make a rewarding family activity. Those sponsored by the local obedience clubs are the most fun and usually have the best instructors. Classes range from beginning dog training, which is helpful for all dog owners, to more advanced classes which prepare the dog for obedience competition.

Educating your dog starts the moment you bring your puppy home and lasts throughout your dog's life. Communicating with and training your dog will help build a strong and satisfying bond of friendship.

Additional resources that are helpful in educating your dog are: *Mother Knows Best: The Natural Way to Train Your Dog*, by Carol Lea Benjamin (New York: Howell Book House, 1985); *Dog Behavior: Why Dogs Do What They Do*, by Ian Dunbar (Neptune, N.J.: T.F.H. Publications, Inc., 1979); *Understanding Your Dog*, by Michael Fox (New York: Bantam Books, 1981); and *How to be Your Dog's Best Friend* by Monks of New Skete (Boston: Little, Brown, 1978).

CHAPTER 8

Welcome Home!

CONGRATULATIONS! You have done your research, taken your time, and made your choice, and now your new dog is coming home. You may have picked a worthy shelter stray, a playful puppy, or an adult purebred, but whatever your choice, this dog is soon to become a special member of your family. However, there are a few last minute steps to take in order to ensure a long, rewarding relationship for you and your new canine friend.

A checklist is in order so that no points are left unattended. For example, making your house and yard dog-proof can prevent canine personality problems and your loss of temper. Finding the right veterinarian, picking the right name, and integrating your new dog with children or other family pets paves the way for a well-adjusted, healthy new pet.

BEFORE THE DOG ARRIVES

1. Obtain a dog bed (pillow or den/crate).

2. Have bowls (food and water), leash, collar, Nylabone (or rawhide bone).

3. Get a supply of food.

4. Walk through your yard and make sure that doors and gates are secure, that there are no holes under fences, and so on.

5. Interview and select a veterinarian; make an appointment for an examination which includes all vaccinations.

6. Investigate obedience training courses or puppy socialization groups.

7. Look into the purchase of a book about dogs.

8. Make plans to get a dog license.

DOG-PROOFING YOUR HOUSE

Your new dog will be curious about everything! Dogs investigate by smelling and tasting. Don't forget that puppies are great chewers. Puppies chew more than adult dogs because of teething. If you have a teething puppy, it may enjoy chewing on ice cubes or a frozen cloth. Make sure that dog-harmful materials such as paint, detergents, antifreeze, and pesticides are safely put away. Check for electrical cords which might cause electrocution. Provide a chew toy such as a Nylabone or rawhide bone. (Real bones are not good for dogs, as they can splinter and cause serious intestinal problems.) If you don't want your canine to chew on your slippers or socks, keep them out of sight! From the moment it enters the house, your dog is learning what it can and cannot do, so don't offer it objects that you don't want it to enjoy chewing.

A few extra pointers to consider: Young puppies that have just left their mothers may be comforted by a ticking clock wrapped in a towel during the first few nights. Make certain your puppy does not have access to a pool; a puppy can drown if it falls into the water and has had no previous swimming experience.

THE BEST TIME FOR HOMECOMING

The first few days your dog is at home set the pattern for its adjustment into the home and family; this period is particularly crucial with a young puppy. The ideal time for bringing your dog home is right before the weekend, so you and your whole family can be with the dog and teach it the ground rules. Even better—if it can be arranged—is during a vacation, when the family is at home for several days or weeks in a row.

When your dog comes home, show it the location of its water dish; make certain a fresh supply of water is available at all times. Take it outside so it can get used to all the new smells; indicate the place where you want it to eliminate. Stay with it, and if by chance it does go, praise it immediately. You are already off to a good start with housetraining!

Talk to your dog in a gentle way and introduce it to each member of the family. If you have children, make certain they understand that the dog will need time to get used to its new space. Emphasize that the dog should be allowed to rest after playtime. If your dog is not going to have a den for its bed, confine it to a small area of the house when you first leave it alone. Even an adult dog needs time to get into the routine of going outside, and until it does, this limits the "mistakes" to an area that you have selected.

NAMING YOUR DOG

One of the first things a dog learns once it arrives home is its name. If you have children, naming the dog can be an enjoyable family project. If you are going to show your dog, you may wish to choose a name that goes well with your surname, as you could be reading them together in print someday! (Obedience clubs often list both names when giving out awards, i.e., Silver Medal to Johmar Wood or Gold Medal to Muffin Post.)

After selecting a name, begin to teach it to respond when called. The best time to start this lesson is at mealtime. Take a piece of food in your hand, say your dog's name and the word "come." When your puppy comes, offer the food. Do this several times during the first few meals and your dog will be eager to respond. You can also do this exercise just before your dog goes out to play. In this way, your dog learns that when it responds to its name, it will get to do something fun.

INTRODUCING A NEW DOG TO AN OLDER ONE

Adding to your canine family can help avoid boredom and loneliness for an "only" dog. But you need to plan the introduction so the older dog does not view the new one as an intruding rival. The best choice of dog in this situation is a puppy; if this is not an option, then a member of the opposite sex or another female dog would also be good choices. (The most difficult combination is two male dogs, because of their need to dominate.)

Here are some suggestions that will make the introduction of the two dogs a little easier:

1. Several weeks before you bring home the new dog, make sure that the older one is in good health and that obedience training is up to date. You need to feel confident that you can control the resident dog before you begin training the new one. Remember that the older dog will teach the younger one everything it knows, so be sure that what it knows is what you want taught!

2. All dogs are territorial, so the initial introduction should take place on neutral ground, such as another yard or a park. Have someone else take charge of the new pet while you hold the old one. Let the dogs sniff each other and play together before bringing them home.

3. For the first few days, keep the dogs in separate quarters when you are absent so that each has its own territory. Play with both dogs; if there is some minor growling or snapping, ignore it at first. If this behavior becomes more serious, correct it. When the resident dog responds well to the new one, reward it with praise and treats.

4. Make sure both dogs get enough exercise. This serves as an outlet for aggressive behavior and gives them an opportunity to enjoy an activity together. Be generous with treats for a few days so the dogs associate food and fun with being together.

5. Be patient! Don't let the dogs know that you are concerned. Communicate that you expect them to get along with each other and soon they will.

THE FIRST VETERINARY VISIT

Soon after your dog arrives, arrange an appointment for a veterinary examination. Make the first visit a pleasant one (bring treats and a bone along) so your new dog will associate a doctor's visit with reward and fun. If you have any questions about your pet's nutrition, health, or behavior, write them down ahead of time. Your dog's doctor is an excellent resource and can be a supportive lifelong friend for your pet.

OBEDIENCE TRAINING

Dogs, like children, need limits and education in order to develop emotional security. If you acquire a puppy, arrange for a socialization class. If your dog is older than six months, it is ready for obedience training. Books on dog behavior and specific breeds can supplement the school training program.

ENJOY! ENJOY! ENJOY!

You have followed the steps described in this book and chosen the best dog for you. However, keep your Dog File and refer to it as you enter different stages of your dog's life. For example, if you add another dog to your family in the future, your research will be ready for you! For now, enjoy your dog, show it lots of love and affection. Like all good friendships, this one requires time, attention, and love. Make a special time to be with your dog every day. Playing with it, exercising it, and conversing with it will build a strong, longlasting bond between you. In turn, let your dog give you all the love and protection that it can. The end result will be a tail-wagging four-footed friend who will look at you with adoring eyes that say, "Thank you for picking me!"

PART TWO

SPECIAL DOGS FOR SPECIAL PEOPLE

CHAPTER 9

Understanding Service Dogs

Tom and Anita Henderson bought a six-month-old German shepherd named Bismarck after their home was robbed. They believed that Bismarck would protect their home and also provide companionship for their eight-year-old son Dennis. The breeder insisted that German shepherds were "natural" guard dogs and so the Hendersons took home their new pet with high hopes.

But Bismarck did not turn out to be what they had expected. Instead of barking at the doorbell, he turned to the Hendersons for protection or ran cowering to another room. Vacuum cleaners and loud birds frightened him. He had never been around children and so he avoided Dennis. At the end of the first week, a dog trainer diagnosed Bismarck as "shy," a condition probably caused by spending too little time with people during his puppy months. The prognosis was that he could become more outgoing with training, but that it was unlikely he would ever become a reliable watchdog. Angry and disappointed, the Hendersons returned the dog to the breeder.

Selecting and living with a working dog requires careful consideration. The owner must choose the dog carefully and be able to control such an independent animal. Before making the decision to get a dog for protection, you can learn much about this type of dog from the police K-9 units which train and use protection dogs.

To understand police dogs, it is important to understand Schutzhund training. This training is a German sport which encompasses obedience work, tracking, and aggressive behavior, taking advantage of the dog's natural instincts. Although it is an ideal preparation for police work, many people have their dogs train and compete to keep them sharp for home protection. A Schutzhund trained dog will attack and bite on command.

THE LOS ANGELES POLICE DEPARTMENT K-9 UNIT

The police sergeant introduced me to his "partner," Friday, who promptly lay down on the floor and fell asleep. Sergeant Mooring leaned over and stroked his partner's ear as he explained, "He is obsessed with his job, but when he gets a chance to relax, it's all four paws on the ground."

Friday, a four-year-old German shepherd, is one of fifteen working dogs of the Los Angeles Police Department (LAPD). With the exception of one Rottweiler (donated to the department), the unit is composed of imported German shepherds. These members of the K-9 unit search out robbery, rape, and murder suspects and, in the process, save the police department time, money, and lives. The ten dogs in the department in 1987 made 1500 searches and caught 450 felony suspects.

Sergeant Mooring is one of two officers who started the K-9 unit in 1980. He is a Los Angeles native and familiar with shepherds. Today, each of the fifteen policemen who make up the human side of the K-9 unit has a twenty-four-hour-a-day four-footed partner. Off-hours, the dogs live at home with their police partners and families. In fact, it is mandatory that each family provide its dog with a covered kennel, six feet by twelve feet, where it can rest during off-hours. (Because of the long work day, many dogs sleep ten hours a day.)

The dogs begin their ten-week training program at eighteen months. Occasionally one of the men will introduce his own puppy for K-9 work. If the puppy is approved, it is taught by both human trainers and veteran dogs. The unit trains its own dogs and has well-trained handlers. It usually takes three to six months for the close bonding between policeman and adult canine partner to develop. This bond is crucial since dogs and men must often save each other in life-and-death situations.

Sergeant Mooring tells me that policemen often prefer a canine partner to a human one because they know the dog's limitations and can therefore predict the dog's behavior. This is not always the case with a human partner. In addition, the dogs don't have personal worries or family problems.

SELECTING THE RIGHT POLICE DOG

Officer Donn Yarnell is chief trainer for the LAPD K-9 unit. He has been a member of the police department for seventeen years and has been training the K-9 corps for eight of those years. He selects the corps of German shepherds during regular trips to Bavaria. Yarnell believes that American-bred shepherds do not have the instincts for police work that Germany's dogs possess.

"I look for raw instincts when I pick out a dog. I want a dog with the drive to fight and hunt. The candidate must have a pack drive, i.e., the willingness to conform to the leader of the pack which, in this case, is the policeman who will train and become partners with the dog." Yarnell doesn't match dog to police partner; he matches policeman to dog.

Yarnell looks at dogs aged eighteen months to three and a half years at various Schutzhund clubs and German police schools. When Yarnell selects a puppy, he looks for confidence, an outgoing personality, nice conformation (to avoid health problems, especially hip problems), and self-motivation (puppies which investigate new things, pick up the leash and play with it, and so on). His favorite in a litter is not the most dominant "alpha" male. He usually picks number two or three in the hierarchy. (If you choose the top puppy, you will fight him all his life, whereas numbers two and three are a bit more submissive.)

Yarnell points out that males tend to be more independent. It's harder to find an alpha female, but when you do, she's usually a great choice! You can recognize an alpha female puppy by her herding instinct; she will be alert as she pushes and herds the other puppies around, just like a mother. As a rule, the female puppy does not vie to be the pack leader.

As far as home protection dogs are concerned, Yarnell's experience is that German shepherds imported from Germany or with German bloodlines are the best. He believes that the American Doberman can be a deterrent to robbers, but ultimately is not a good protection dog, while the German Dobermans are too hard to train. He also considers the Bouvier a fairly good protection breed. The Belgian Malinois has potential for home protection. With a responsible owner, the pit bull, which is used for police narcotics work, is also an excellent choice for home protection.

According to David Reaver, who has been involved with dog training since 1972, two breeds are the most reliable for police training: the German shepherd and the Belgian Malinois. Once a dog has been selected, Reaver's next concern is with its physical health: The dog must show no indication of hip dysplasia. Unlike German breeders, who routinely X-ray their shepherds, Dutch breeders do not X-ray the Malinois. So before a Malinois is selected, Reaver insists on a hip X ray. If its hips are good, Reaver checks the dog's I.D. tattoos against its registration papers, to make sure he has the right dog.

He then runs the dogs through a preselection evaluation with exercises similar to the actual training course in Adlerhorst. He wants a dog with speed and alertness which is totally unafraid of the sound of gunfire. Another important characteristic is a high degree of prey drive, which is the instinct that drives a hungry dog to hunt in the wild. Of course, the intense vigilance, speed, and determination to get food or prey need to be channeled into proper police work. Reaver points out that even though the dogs perform strenuous and intense work, they must also like people. Off-duty dogs live with their partners, who often have a spouse and children. The dog must be as confident and comfortable in this home environment as it is in police work.

TESTING

As mentioned, trainers of dogs in police units look for certain qualities. Most often, these qualities are discovered by putting the dog through a battery of tests. Some of the tests LAPD trainer Yarnell uses are described below.

THE STAKE TEST

This test is done in two parts. In the first part, the dog is tied to a stake for five minutes, out of the sight of people and not on the dog's training ground. (It is important to test the dog on neutral ground, where the dog's instincts, rather than its previous training, will show through.) The tester makes his presence known from a concealed location and approaches the dog, sometimes fast, sometimes with a slow, jerky motion. As he approaches the dog, he stares at it, then looks away. He carries a stick, and as he gets closer, he holds it up and threatens the dog with it.

This test tells you how much fortitude the dog has. If you watch its body, you can spot different responses. For example, a submissive dog may show signs of insecurity, such as raising the hair on its back or giving a high-pitched bark. If a dog wants to warn you rather than fight you, it will show its teeth, turn sideways, look away, and maybe even run away. The fighting dog, which is the most appropriate type for police work, will challenge you and try to pull off the line to get at you in the full fight mode.

The second part of the test, withdrawing the challenge, is as important as the first. Here the tester stops, puts down the stick, kneels down, and looks away for twenty or thirty seconds. (He is imitating the behavior of a submissive wolf, indicating he no longer is offering a challenge to the dog.) Then he calls the dog's name and asks it to come, then pets and praises it.

If a dog has the right temperament for police work, it will recover from the challenge and allow you to pet it.

THE WEAPONS TEST

While the dog is performing its Schutzhund work, two rounds of gunshot are fired. Then later, when the dog is on the leash, several more are fired. The dog's reactions are observed carefully—a good police dog is not afraid of gunfire.

THE SLEEVE TEST

In this test, a tester wearing very thick, "bite-proof" sleeves hides and waits for the dog to find him. When the dog finds the man, it should bark or bite his arm, preferably without looking at the handler. The tester watches this exercise carefully: The police dog needs to be self-motivated and not dependent on handler cues.

THE TEMPERAMENT TEST

Testing the dog for temperament is done by running a hand over the dog's body, much as judges do in breed rings. The tester is interested in whether or not the dog accepts this.

THE RETRIEVING TEST

This is an additional test, which is not crucial to police work but is an indication of how easily the dog can be trained. In this test, the handler throws a ball and watches the dog's enthusiasm for bringing it back.

TRAINING—CHANNELING THE DOG'S INSTINCTS

When training a dog, it is important to leave it wanting to do more. In other words, train your dog until it is tired; you want your dog to *want* to work, not to *have* to work. Five to ten minutes of good work is worth its weight in performance. One handler mistake is trying to get the upper hand with the dog. The dog needs a sense of self-confidence, and it acquires this when the trainer shows it respect, so both dog and handler trust each other. There must be a true human-dog partnership. In addition, training should be fast and fun for the dog.

Adlerhorst International trains officers and canine partners for over eighty law enforcement agencies, which include police, sheriffs, and narcotics departments. A 160-hour basic course for police dog work teaches general obedience skills such as retrieving, scaling a wall, and moving through an obstacle course similar to those in marine boot camp. Once the dog has acquired these foundation skills, it moves on to the next level of training, which includes surveillance, searching for a suspect, transporting prisoners, and escape prevention. Narcotic detection training teaches a dog to search for four different drugs and to avoid misleading scents.

MATCHING DOG AND HANDLER

Once an officer has been accepted into the K-9 program, he or she must be matched with the right dog. The process begins with the officer; he or she receives three different dogs to work with. (Dogs are graded "good," "very good," and "excellent," according to their skill and ability to handle stress.) Although all dogs have Schutzhund training, some have more dominant personalities than others. An alpha dog (one which wants to be top dog and take charge) requires a strong, confident officer. This kind of dog tests its partner immediately; if the handler shows any fear, the match will most likely fail. On the other hand, a sensitive dog should not be placed with an officer who is too dominant and may be insensitive to the dog's personality. If the officer tries to dominate the dog too quickly, it may react negatively. When the new handlers try out the three dog candidates, both dog and officer use body language to adjust to each other. Invariably, one of the three dogs will feel the most comfortable to the officer and vice versa; thus a match is made.

CANINE CUSTOMS OFFICERS

At the Canine Enforcement Training Center in Front Royal, Virginia, which has been training dogs since 1971, nine "narcotics" dogs have just completed a twelve-week drug detection course and are ready to begin work. These canine graduates will be shipped to ports of entry throughout the United States where they will be put to work sniffing out illegal drugs which may be hidden in vehicles, ships, and planes. These "customs inspectors" save the government time and money as they help the U. S. fight the war against drugs.

Instructors from the training centers look for dogs that enjoy retrieving and will respond to a behavior modification program in which the reward is play. They look for a dog that is "headstrong," one that always wants to be out at the end of the leash searching. Dogs must be at least one year old. Ninety-eight percent of dog applicants come from humane societies and local pounds. Trainers have found that mixed breeds from shelters perform better than purebreds brought up in homes and kennels. (The instructor describes these dogs as "streetwise," in that they are used to the smells of the real world environment.) Mixed breeds combining Labrador retriever, German shepherd, golden retriever, and German short-haired pointer are the most successful canines in this program. Trainers search for a dog that loves to play. Most likely they will select a dog whose enthusiasm for chasing a ball and retrieving it wears out the tester; it is this "play drive" which will be used in training the dogs for detection work.

After a medical checkup (which includes hip analysis), the dogs begin a twelve-week on-the-job training session. Initially they are matched to a handler by size, with bigger dogs going with larger instructors; however, changes are usually made during the first week, as compatibility between partners becomes clearer. For example, a dog may be sensitive to a loud voice and thus will work better for a handler who speaks softly.

Unlike most working dogs, these dogs do not receive basic obedience training because the Customs Service is only interested in canines who will search for drugs with persistence and enthusiasm. Behavior modification techniques are used; the reward is always a game of tug-of-war with a towel. Within three days, the dog learns to search for his toy (the rolled-up towel) in order to get a chance to play. The next step is attaching a canvas bag of narcotics or explosives to the towel. From this exercise, the dog learns that the ability to sniff out the drug or explosives will lead to his favorite game of tug-of-war.

The remainder of the session is devoted to learning eleven search patterns. For example, the dogs practice retrieving drugs in luggage moving on a conveyor belt; in mail bags stored in vehicles; in cargo ship boxes. They are trained to sniff out drugs in strange areas, such as up ladders and underneath vehicles. They learn to discriminate between interesting food odors and the smell of a sealed-up bag of drugs. Those dogs which pass the course are shipped to ports of entry. Occasionally, a dog does not have enough play drive to pass the program. Luckily, the Canine Enforcement Center has a waiting list of people ready to adopt the dogs who cannot graduate.

Unlike most service dogs, these canine detectors do not live with their handlers but rather in Customs Department kennels. One reason for this is to reinforce their motivation for viewing their work as play. Canine detection careers average nine years; some dogs have worked for twelve. After retirement, dogs usually live with their handlers or are placed in homes. Further information on this program can be obtained from U. S. Customs Service, Canine Enforcement Training Center, Front Royal, Virginia; telephone (202) 566-8188.

Do You Want a
Home Protection Dog?

There is little difference between the temperament of a police dog and a good protection dog for your home. However, a personal protection dog is often less aggressive than a police dog. Most people seeking a home protection dog will not import one from Europe. Unfortunately, many guard dogs bred and sold in this country are "fear biters," which means they will react with indiscriminate aggression out of a feeling of insecurity. It is essential that you do not choose such a dog for your home; a trained working dog should protect you only on command.

If you are selecting a dog *primarily* for home protection, consider the following tips:

1. Look for good health and strong hips (insist on an X ray or a medical certificate).

2. The dog should be at least eighteen months old. (When protection is the paramount concern, serious buyers tend to choose a proven adult rather than taking their chances with selecting and training a puppy.)

3. Look for a friendly, sociable dog that responds well to you.

CHOOSING A PROTECTION PUPPY

When choosing a puppy from a litter, start by investigating the breeder and checking on the dog's parents. Visit the litter at two and three weeks. Observe the puppies. Look for the most outgoing (or more mischievous) puppy. If you are lucky enough to find a litter with an alpha female, she's a good choice. If you select a male, remember you are better off not choosing the alpha but selecting the number two or three puppy, as it will best respond to your training. Carefully studying the dog's conformation is the best way to predict if the puppy is structurally sound.

Watching a puppy move will give you an opportunity to observe its gait. Occasionally you will see one that walks like a miniature adult. That puppy will make a good-moving adult working dog. Pick up the puppies and see how they respond. A little playful wiggle is good. A lack of wiggle is too passive. If the puppy is too sensitive to allow you to hold it, it is not a good candidate. Run your hand over the body of the puppy to see if it is body-sensitive.

Separate all the puppies and see which is independent enough to play and which has to return to the others. Remember: The time of day that you observe is important. Don't evaluate the litter after the puppies have eaten or at naptime.

Proper training will be your responsibility. With a puppy, you are getting one-third raw instincts and two-thirds dependence on environment and training.

TRAINING YOUR PROTECTION DOG

Whether you choose a puppy or an adult protection dog, you will need to do some training before the dog will work for you. Initially, you and the dog must go through basic obedience training. This is available at recreation parks or through local obedience clubs and some humane societies. Once the dog has mastered obedience work, advanced working skills can be learned by joining a local Schutzhund club. Over 160 Schutzhund clubs work with dogs and hold competition events where both dog and master can practice their skills. Information on the location of one of these clubs in your area can be found by writing to Kay Koerner at United Schutzhund Clubs of America, 1926 Hillman Avenue, Belmont, California 94002; telephone (415) 591-1917.

Semi-Protection Dogs

Not everyone needs a fully trained protection dog. The time and responsibility this type of dog requires may not suit your lifestyle or needs. However, the dog's ability to hear and smell a threatening intruder makes it a natural burglar alarm system. So you may wish to choose a puppy or dog that will alert you to intruders by vigorous barking.

When the dog barks at strangers, be sure to praise it. (With obedience work, you can also teach your dog to sit or stay down when your friends arrive, so it will not bark continually.) A dog that barks when you are not home discourages strangers and the mere presence of a large dog can deter intruders. A "Beware of Dog" sign on your fence can also discourage unwanted visitors. You will always have to spend some time working with your dog to encourage its natural territorial instinct, but it is well worth the feeling of security that the dog offers you and your family.

CHAPTER 10

Seeing-Eye Dogs

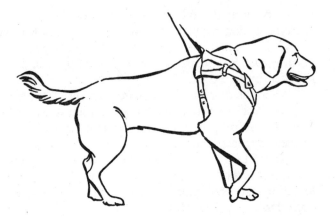

GUIDE DOGS FOR the blind are probably the best-known service animals. During World War I, dogs were trained as messengers and guides for rescue work. Following the war, Germany trained dogs to help their blinded veterans and civilians. It was soon discovered that guide dogs offered the blind an opportunity to lead independent lives. Training facilities are now established throughout the world.

In opting to use a guide dog, the blind person makes a life choice that affects more than just his or her mobility. A guide dog provides physical, social, and psychological benefits. Studies show that blind people who have dogs feel safer, and have increased physical confidence and stamina and greater self-esteem. The relationship offers the blind person a feeling of self-respect, as the dog shows no judgment about the disability. In addition, the dog owner is more comfortable relying on a dog than he or she is asking for the same help from a person. The ability of the dog and owner to communicate verbally and nonverbally offers the owner emotional satisfaction and stability.

The first seeing-eye guide dog center in the United States was established in 1929 by Dorothy Harrison Eustis, a breeder of German shepherds. There are now eleven guide dog training centers in the country. They vary in methodology, funding, and selection of dogs. Most schools depend on private funding, charging no fee (or a minimal one) to the guide dog recipient.

There are 500,000 legally blind persons in the United States. Of this total, about 10 percent, or 50,000, are potential users of guide dogs. Some of the other 90 percent simply don't care for dogs, or prefer to use a cane. Others have complicating conditions, such as brittle bones, diabetes, or severe obesity.

Also, a blind person must be older than sixteen to be assigned a dog. But for those who are suited to using a guide dog, it can change their lives.

Using a guide dog greatly increases the freedom of a blind person who has already developed skills with a cane. It is the blind person who directs the dog and not vice versa. The master or mistress must sense the flow of traffic and command the dog to cross. Dogs are color-blind and cannot tell the difference between a red and a green light. The dog is trained to enter the street after seeing that it is safe. It is taught that a moving vehicle is a signal to stop and that a stationary vehicle is a signal to proceed.

Because of the complex skills a dog must acquire, training of instructors and guide dogs is not taken lightly. For instance, California has a state law requiring guide dog instructors to complete a three-year apprenticeship at a guide dog school. Then they must pass a state board examination. In training the dogs the instructors learn to simulate blindness (by wearing blindfolds) while walking their dogs on suburban and city streets. Dogs require nearly forty of these walking tours before they are ready to begin instruction with a blind person.

International Guiding Eyes (IGE)

International Guiding Eyes (IGE), which is located in Sylmar, California, accepts applicants from all over the world. They train dogs for blind persons and also for those with multiple handicaps and for the elderly. The dogs are provided at no cost to the recipient, along with a specially designed harness and one month of training at the IGE school. When dog and applicant are matched, they must undergo a twenty-eight-day live-in training session. By the end of the first week, the dog transfers its allegiance from the staff instructor to its new master. Each student room has an attached outdoor run for the dog. The guide dog teams work both inside and outside the center so the students learn to take their dogs into restaurants and shopping malls, through revolving doors, and on buses, cars, and airplanes.

Rick Boggs, who had been self-sufficient with his cane, was talked into acquiring a guide dog. He liked IGE's program, but the training period with his new dog, Brent, was frustrating and too challenging. Like most German shepherds, Brent had the intelligence and initiative to make his own decisions and liked having his own way. The same sensitivity that could make Brent an exceptional guide dog also made him a difficult student. One day during the fourth week of the IGE live-in training course, Brent went on strike: No matter how much praise Rick gave him, the dog would not perform. Rick returned to the dorm with his dog and cried.

He and Brent were scheduled for busy street practice the next day and Rick was scared and discouraged. That night, he decided to give up and leave the training. The next morning, Rick remembered the beginning of his friendship with the dog. Brent had been uninterested in Rick and had pined for his trainer of five months. Rick had even had to sit with him to get him to eat. Rick imagined how Brent would be returned to the kennel if he quit, and he knew how hard that would be on the dog. He changed his mind: He realized that he could quit the school but he couldn't quit on his dog. The trainer worked with Rick on how to hang back and let Brent move out and how to make his voice more enthusiastic. Eventually the two learned to work together. Brent even helped Rick get a talking part in a documentary on guide dogs.

SELECTION PROCESS

Originally, female German shepherds were used as guide dogs because of their intelligence and ability to learn quickly. The shepherds' possession of these qualities, however, also means that they tend to be more dominant, assertive, and sensitive to a changing environment. In addition, their tendency towards loyalty to one master made the necessary changes in ownership—from puppy raiser to school instructor to disabled master—emotionally difficult.

Today, the breeds used are not exclusively shepherds. For example, 70 percent of IGE's dogs are Labrador retrievers, 20 percent are golden retrievers, 8 percent are German shepherds, and 2 percent are Border collies or flat-coated retrievers. Shepherds which accept training can develop into good guide dogs. The Labrador is a willing, loving, adaptable dog and has good initiative. Aside from some occasional stubbornness, it works well, gets along with families, and is easy to groom. Golden retrievers are also loving and eager to work, but they are more sensitive than the Labradors. If they are pushed too fast during training, their confidence breaks down and they lose their initiative.

Ninety percent of IGE's puppies are bred at the center by carefully selected brood bitches and studs of three to five generations. The school breeds for such traits as initiative, healthy structure, strength, size, intelligence, concentration, voice responsiveness, even temperament, tolerance of noise, and willingness to work. At eight weeks of age, the puppies are placed with carefully selected puppy raisers.

Puppy raisers are chosen on the basis of the amount of quality time they can spend with a puppy, their interest in bringing up a well-mannered dog, and the availability of children and other socialization experiences. Puppies sleep in their raiser's bedroom and learn basic obedience work. Once a month, the center holds an educational meeting, with emphasis on nutrition, flea control, and obedience work. At eight to ten months, dogs are spayed or neutered. Between twelve and eighteen months, depending on how quickly a dog matures, it returns to the school for intensive training. (Shepherds are usually trained at a later age because they mature more slowly.)

TRAINING THE GUIDE DOG

When the dogs are returned to school they begin a rigorous four- to six-month training program. If the dog has sound structure and good health, it is assigned to one instructor who will work with it throughout the training period. Two out of ten dogs are rejected at this point because of hip dysplasia. Dogs that have not learned basic obedience commands from the puppy raiser are taught these skills before they move into guide work training.

When guide dog training begins, all the puppies play in a central yard together twice a day while the instructors observe the way they interact; for example, they notice whether each dog is passive, dominant, or aggressive. This information helps staff members evaluate the dog's personality so they can consider which one best matches a given disabled candidate. The instructor then takes the dog out (on a long leash) into the town and watches how it reacts to buses, trucks, cars, and people. The trainer notes if the dog is eager to please and its level of initiative to do so. He or she watches to see if the dog will walk in front and with what levels of timidity and concentration. The trainer observes if the dog is interested in sniffing, or looking into windows, or if it walks straight ahead. He or she notices what kind of judgments the dog makes. For instance, when a parent approaches with a stroller, does the dog find a way around it?

Basic guide work requires intense concentration. The dog is taught to walk in a straight line at the trainer's left side and to stay in the center of the sidewalk, not hugging the curb. It learns how to stop at the curb, make left and right turns, and go around obstacles. The dog is initially trained with a soft harness without a handle. (The handle training comes later, as some sensitive dogs find it restrictive; it is especially important not to scare a dog with too much pressure early on in the training.) During the third month of instruction, the dog learns to be aware of traffic. It is taught to stop when it sees a car and to continue in a straight line when the car passes.

By the time the dog completes the training course, it has also learned what the staff calls "respectful disobedience." This is when the dog uses its experience and knowledge to disobey a command that would cause danger to the owner. For instance, the owner may issue the command "forward," not knowing there is a moving vehicle or an open manhole cover ahead. Since the blind person never walks ahead of the dog, this "disobedience" can be life-saving.

MATCHING THE DOG TO THE RECIPIENT

Students are carefully screened to assure that they will be successful in using a guide dog. Before acceptance, they must complete an application that asks for such information as occupation, primary method of transportation used, history as dog owner, and home and yard conditions. If the applicant is local, he or she may be interviewed at home. The staff specifically want to know if any family member would object to having a dog in the house. The applicant must understand the guide dog's limitations, so part of the application procedure includes an orientation and a mobility evaluation that reveals the person's level of independence and indicates his or her aptitude for working with a guide dog. A guide dog cannot be expected to replace a sighted person who may have been the disabled person's guide before the introduction of the canine partner.

About six weeks before the student arrives at the training center, the instructors make the crucial matching decision. They look at the dogs available and make note of their traits. Then they look at the applicant's needs and abilities. Instructors take into account a student's size, pace, temperament, and preferences. (Applicants are asked if there is a particular breed they do not want.)

Eighteen-year-old Jean was 5'4", 114 pounds, and needed a dog on the small side to accompany her to school. She had some useful residual vision and could handle a less capable dog. Because she spent a good deal of time in class, she also needed a well-settled dog that was not too energetic. The trainers went over the list of available dogs and finally matched her with a sensitive and quiet golden retriever.

In another instance, Mary, who was sixty-eight, was ready for her second guide dog. Her first one was a high-energy retriever which had worked well because Mary not only worked part-time but was also active in community work. But when Mary retired, her situation changed: She needed a less energetic pup. So, after some consultation, the IGE trainers switched dogs and gave her a calmer, less energetic Labrador.

Matching dog and applicant is the most difficult part of guide dog training. All factors are considered carefully. And while incompatibility between student and dog can occur, in practice it is rare.

The working life of a guide dog is between eight and twelve years. If the dog becomes too old to work properly or becomes physically disabled itself, the owner is allowed to keep the dog as a pet while obtaining a new one to act as a guide.

International Guiding Eye, which operates solely on private, tax-deductible donations, is located at 13445 Glenoaks Boulevard, Sylmar, California 91342; telephone (818) 362-5834.

CHAPTER 11

Hearing-Ear Dogs

J UST AS SEEING-EYE dogs are taught to provide "eyes" to the blind, hearing-ear dogs provide "ears" to the deaf. Trained to listen for and to assist the hearing-impaired, these dogs alert their owners to specific sounds in their environments.

In 1975, Agnes McGrath, founder of International Hearing Dogs, Inc., became the first person to train dogs for the deaf in a program started by the Minnesota Society for the Prevention of Cruelty to Animals. Since that time, training centers all over the United States have been training dogs from humane societies and placing them with deaf owners.

When choosing a new dog for "signal work," the most important trait is temperament: The hearing-ear dog should want to please its master but must not be overly submissive. It should be friendly to strangers but not become distracted from its work. It should be protective but never attempt to bite. The dog's natural intelligence, learning ability, and hearing are crucial. Hearing-ear trainers are always searching shelters for friendly, confident, eager-to-please pups with an aptitude for hearing-ear work. Dogs which qualify can be any breed—mixed or pure—and are usually between six and twenty-four months of age. They are generally of small to medium size, primarily because they must live indoors and because many signals are given by touching or jumping up on the owner. Trainers at the Riverside program (which operates in connection with the Riverside, California Humane Society) feel that Shetland sheepdogs, German shepherds, Doberman pinschers, and retrievers learn signal work quickly. Trainers at the SF/SPCA have found that terriers, shelties, corgis, spaniel mixes, and poodles often fit this type of work well. Both males and females are trainable; most of the dogs are altered before placement. Dogs which require extensive grooming are usually avoided. Dogs under one year learn faster than older ones, but some well-motivated older dogs are able to learn how to do the signal work too. Dogs which bark continually behind the fence at the shelter probably would not tolerate the confinement when their new owners leave them at home. Dogs are observed to see if windup toys or noisemakers interest them. Sometimes trainers will play a tape of a sound. If the dog gets frustrated and tries to find the source, it is suitable for hearing-ear work. If a dog is worked regularly, it can be active for six to ten years.

There are two hearing-ear programs in California that are worthy of note.

THE MARY ANN SALEM COMPANION ANIMAL PROGRAM FOR THE DEAF

Eight dogs and their owners sat in an evening training class of the Mary Ann Salem Companion Animal Program for the Deaf at the Riverside Humane Society. The eight student dogs were learning how to alert their human partners to common household sounds, as their owners were either completely or partially deaf. I watched as a black-and-white Border collie named Juju ran to Cecilia, his owner, and jumped up and put his front paws on her arm, alerting her to the sound of a ringing telephone. Then he led her to a large wooden box where the telephone was located and received a treat and a hug as a reward. For Cecilia, a part-time secretary, this was her fourth week of training with Juju. Next to Cecilia sat a young couple with a one-year-old baby. They were training Honey, an eight-month sheltie. When Honey heard the baby cry, she got excited, circled twice and then ran to nuzzle the baby's mother. In her four weeks of training, Honey had learned how to alert her owners to the baby crying, a knock on the door, and the sound of the fire alarm. At the end of the sixteen-week course, the dogs which passed performance requirements received a certification card showing they had been trained as official signal dogs.

Juju and Honey are two of the sixty hearing-ear dogs trained annually by Karen Detterich, community services coordinator of the Riverside animal companion programs. The majority of signal dogs are chosen from homeless strays in the shelter and are more than willing to learn how to contribute to the lives of their new owners. In some cases, dog trainees are pets of the hearing-impaired who are being retrained as hearing-ear dogs.

Most hearing-ear programs first train the dog and then match it to the new owner. The Salem Companion Animal Program for the Deaf is unique in that the hearing-impaired person is taught how to train his or her own dog. When a dog is trained by its owner, it is more responsive to its master's special needs. Also, the dog benefits from "on-the-job training" in its future home. The hearing-impaired person develops a stronger bond with the pet by working closely with it, and later enjoys the pride of accomplishment when training is complete.

Another feature of the Riverside program is that puppies are placed quite young. The puppy candidates are selected at between seven and sixteen weeks; the hearing-impaired owner must then learn how to housebreak and correct the puppy. The young dog must learn the skills needed for frequent contact with people and outings to public places, where it must be familiar with sounds in the community. Along with this socialization process, "playtraining" games teach the puppy to be sound-aware and eager to learn. This early training prevents the development of bad habits, so that when the dog is between five and eight months old, it is ready to start its formal weekly three-hour class.

Dogs are first taught basic obedience work. Then the owner selects a minimum of four sounds for the dog to learn, such as: an alarm clock, a kitchen timer, a smoke alarm, an intruder, a dropped object, a baby crying, a telephone, a door knock, or sirens. All of the commands use voice and/or special hand signals. After the dog completes training, it becomes a certified signal dog. In almost every state a certified signal dog cannot be denied housing or excluded from entrance into restaurants or businesses.

Karen Detterich, who has been involved in the selection and training of signal dogs since 1981, finds that matching the right dog to the right person is very challenging. Before she picks the dog, she has an in-home interview with the applicant so she can evaluate both the home and the people who will live with the dog. She considers their needs carefully. For example, some applicants have an emotional preference for a particular breed. Many of the hearing-impaired live in rental housing and need smaller dogs. Detterich tries to balance the activity level of dog and applicant. If an applicant is unusually nervous, she looks for a calm dog. For a quiet person, she seeks a more outgoing dog. If there are children in the family, she must find a dog which would be compatible with them.

When picking a dog at the shelter, Detterich looks for the dog that tries to get eye contact. She evaluates the potential dog candidate to see if it can get excited and then settle down quickly. When possible, she will place a puppy in the home immediately so it can develop a bond to its master and avoid shyness and fearful behavior.

THE SAN FRANCISCO SPCA
HEARING DOG PROGRAM

The San Francisco SPCA also has a program of providing signal dogs to the hearing-impaired. Since 1978, this program has rescued over three hundred homeless dogs, trained them, and placed them with hearing-impaired citizens in California. According to Ralph Dennard, director of the Hearing Dog Program for the SF/SPCA, any person eighteen years or older with a severe hearing loss may be eligible to receive a dog free of charge. Dennard adds that not only does this program help the disabled, but it may be a life-saver for many of the stray animals, since they are rescued and given the opportunity to lead productive and serviceable lives.

To find the best dog, the SF/SPCA trainer walks through the shelter and looks for the dog that jumps up on the gate and wants to make eye contact. This dog is taken out of the kennel and put into the lobby area to see how it reacts to other dogs and people. The trainer looks to see if the dog has difficulty walking or running on a slick surface; signal dogs must move securely from sound to owner. The dog is then walked outside to test its level of confidence around noises and vehicles. The trainers watch to see if the dog likes to walk and whether it pays attention to the trainer or prefers to sniff around. When the dog is instructed to sit, the trainer notices how it tolerates this instruction. The trainer gives the leash a jerk and notices how the dog responds to this kind of stress. Hearing-ear dogs need to be forgiving. If the dog passes all these requirements, it is sent on to the next level: temperament testing.

Temperament testing includes a stress/discomfort test during which the dog is pinched lightly between the toes to see if it bites or otherwise gets angry. Also, it must be subservient enough to allow the tester to place it on its back. (Overly submissive dogs are not desired as they might collapse under the stress of training.) Curiosity is tested by watching the dog's reaction to a pull toy. A play test shows how the dog responds to retrieving. The dog must be eager for treats. This is particularly important because in order for the dog to do well, it must really want rewards. For the last test, the dog gets a chance to hear the sound of a smoke alarm, a whistle, and a timing device. The dog should perk up its ears, sniff, and go over to the sound. This natural curiosity will make training easier. About 45 percent of the dogs evaluated by the SF/SPCA are accepted for training.

The next step for each dog is a thorough medical examination by SF/SPCA veterinarians. Dogs undergo extensive lab studies and blood tests in addition to receiving all necessary vaccinations.

Now, SF/SPCA canine students are ready for training. During the four-month program, each trainer has several dogs which he introduces to "sound" work. The trainers usually communicate using sign language, which is the communication method of choice for about 50 percent of the deaf recipients.

The dog then receives obedience training and sound-keying to the environment. It has daily sessions when it hears a door knock, a telephone ring, a timer, or other home sounds; each time the dog responds correctly, it is given a treat and praise. Soon, the animal learns that responding to the sound is a game with a reward. At certain stages of this learning process, the dog gets "light-line" leash corrections (using a long, light leash that allows the dog a lot of freedom) in the presence of distractions. This is done to help develop a "working attitude" and to spot and eliminate the dogs that fail to adopt such an attitude. At the end of the training the dog is matched to its hearing-impaired partner.

Prospective dog owners are interviewed at an orientation meeting, where the training staff learns all the relevant details about each applicant's lifestyle and home environment. The staff then evaluates the applicant's dog ownership personality. For instance, a confident, dominant dog needs a strong person. A "soft dog" (more sensitive) should not be given to someone with a harsh voice or stern mannerisms. Finally, based on the application, the interview, and sometimes a home visit, the match is made.

The next step is for the team to attend an all-day school in a training center at the SF/SPCA for five days. They practice in apartment settings which include a living room, kitchen, and bedroom with a bed, where dogs learn, for example, to wake up their masters when the alarm goes off. During this period, the dogs learn to work and "hear" with their new partners. The new owners are taught how to maintain a dog's obedience and sound-alert skill, and how to take care of their new companions.

For the first few months after adoption, recipients are asked to file periodic status reports so that the SF/SPCA training staff can evaluate the team's progress and resolve any problems which occur in the dog's new home. Refresher training courses are held periodically.

ADDITIONAL PROGRAMS

The Hearing Ear Dog Program at West Boylston, Massachusetts, was founded in 1976 and is another excellent training center. Dogs in this program, which are also selected from animal shelters, must be healthy, intelligent, eager to please, and curious about sound. The dogs receive four to six months of training, depending on the number of sounds they will need to recognize. Before placement, the new owner receives instruction in the care of the dog. Then dog and owner attend a two-week training program together. The owner is taught how to work with the dog and how to use obedience commands to control the animal. Because many of the deaf cannot speak clearly, the dog is taught to obey hand signals rather than verbal commands. Follow-up help is available after the dog moves into its new home.

Another program is International Hearing Dog, Inc., in Henderson, Colorado. This group, organized in 1979, trains and places dogs in the U.S. and Canada. Support for the program comes from community groups, most notably Silent Partners, which recruits sponsors for the training of individual dogs for the deaf. Sponsors receive a picture of the hearing-ear dog and news of the dog's hearing-impaired master.

Red Acre Farm, established in 1903, was once a location for Boston's retired city work horses. It began its hearing dog program in 1981, as a regional center for the American Humane Association. The dogs are orphans from shelters and go through four to six months of training in basic obedience and sound-awareness. After undergoing an interview, owners are selected and matched with available dogs. Most of the clients are either completely deaf or have a profound hearing loss; some live alone or with a deaf spouse. After the trained dog is brought to the new home, a staff member supervises the dog-human team through the transition.

It is estimated that there are 3.5 to 4 million people with profound hearing loss and another 14 million who suffer hearing loss to a lesser degree. And there are three times as many deaf people as there are blind people in the United States. Luckily, the success rate of the owner–hearing dog pairing is a high one, thanks to consistent owner training and the follow-up programs offered by the various hearing-ear programs. Dogs for the deaf are more than service dogs—they give love and security to their owners. They become members of the family. Bonding with their owners in a relationship of mutual affection, these animals bring a new sense of independence into a soundless existence.

CHAPTER 12

Dogs for the Physically Challenged

THERE WAS SILENCE when I entered the classroom, which was filled with expectant dogs and their expectant masters. Five golden retrievers, two black Labradors, one Border collie, and a Pembroke Welsh corgi lay on the floor, watching quietly. The pups had endured eighteen months of prior training. The head trainer pulled out a list; as he read each dog's name, he presented a leash to a prospective owner. Some leashes were placed in the hands of the students, others needed to be hooked to wheelchairs. This was the first day for preliminary matching—the beginning of a partnership—in which a working dog would offer companionship and guidance to a disabled master.

"Everyone, space out around the room so you can greet your dog and let him hear your greeting," said Anthony, the head trainer. He continued, "The dog will read your voice and your face and can hear your welcome. Remember, we are working as a team, and during this two-week period we may need to exchange your dog with someone else's depending on how well you are matched."

I watched eight-year-old Barry, who has no use of his hands, lean over to nuzzle Olympus with his face. Linda, partially paralyzed by a stroke, put her good arm around her dog and said, "Dakota, you are going to be mine." Because of her condition, it was difficult to understand her words, but Dakota felt Linda's enthusiasm and wagged her tail.

"Love your dogs," repeated Anthony as the wheelchairs moved and the tails wagged.

On the third day of dog training "boot camp," the nine disabled students were learning how to work with their own dogs. These dogs were bred by Canine Companions for Independence (CCI), a nonprofit organization in Santa Rosa, California that breeds and trains working dogs for the disabled. The project is the brainchild of Bonita Bergen, who noticed, while teaching in Turkey, that the handicapped in that country used burros to assist them in their daily routines. When she and her husband returned to the United States, they originated the innovative canine training program.

The nine dogs I observed were almost ready to go home with their new owners. Seven of the dogs were *service* dogs, trained to work for people who have been physically disabled by an accident or other condition, such as polio, cerebral palsy, spinal cord injury, arthritis, stroke, or muscular dystrophy. One was a *signal* dog, trained to alert his hearing-impaired master. The ninth canine was a trained *social* dog, assigned to be a companion to Todd, a ten-year-old autistic boy. As well as functioning as a companion, the dog will help the boy to connect emotionally with other people.

Each of the dogs is familiar with eighty-nine separate commands, but the group has a wide range of personality and proficiency. Like their partners, the dogs have physical and emotional strengths and weaknesses. For example, one enjoys picking up a book and bringing it back to his master, while another, whose personality is more subdued, requires prompting before it retrieves the same object. Some dogs love to pull the wheelchair; others become distracted and even lose confidence if their partner is too uncertain in giving a command. Some need to hear the command only once, while others need more prompting.

Boot camp may be initial training for the disabled owners, but it is actually "college" training for these well-educated dogs. These fifth-generation dogs have been bred and raised for health, temperament, and the skill to do their job.

CCI puppies are placed with foster families at the age of eight weeks. Volunteer families offer their homes for bringing up the puppies in a playful, stimulating, and loving environment. The foster family is interviewed and placed on a waiting list. Keeping the family on the waiting list is one way that CCI can judge the seriousness of the potential foster parents. The puppy must live indoors, sleep in the puppy raiser's bedroom, have a yard with a fence, be fed according to CCI nutritional standards, and take part in an extensive obedience training program. CCI personnel visit the family periodically to make sure that the puppy is being raised according to CCI guidelines.

Placement in good foster homes is important, for it ensures that the impressionable puppy learns to trust, to communicate, to feel secure, to understand acceptable behavior, and to enjoy its initial education. It lives indoors and sleeps in its puppy raiser's bedroom so it will develop the ability to bond and the sense of responsibility that it will be required to offer to its future disabled owner. Often the puppies accompany their foster parents to work or school. They learn to be comfortable in many situations with many different people. The foster family keeps its puppy until it is fifteen to seventeen months old. During this time, guardian and puppy attend regular obedience classes and do daily homework to prepare the dogs for the next step.

BOOT CAMP

During this two-week period, the staff must make the best match between dog and owner while considering each owner's physical and psychological needs. For example, Barry needed a good puller who would also cuddle with him and make him laugh. Linda needed a dog which would give her a feeling of protection. Todd needed a puppy that was outgoing, to keep him from drifting into his own fantasy world.

When the training exercises began, all the dogs were brought into the room on a leash and told to lie down and stay. When the dogs were released, they were allowed to jump up and play with each other or otherwise explore the room. Everyone watched but no one was supposed to speak. Without sound or movement, the dogs found the students boring and ignored them. During this exercise, the participants learned that it takes more than their presence to interest a dog. In the next exercise, a package of moldy cheese was placed outside the door. The students learned how a curious smell attracts a dog's attention. And last, the trainer established contact by petting and talking to the animals. Only then did the dogs become interested in the human participants. During these exercises, the students learned the basic nature of a canine before any training was attempted.

The students moved on and practiced commands with their dogs. The staff watched the interaction between each disabled person and dog closely. Also, they watched the dogs' varied skills and personalities. The trainers look for dogs that will complement the students' strengths and make up for their weaknesses.

At the end of this training day each student was asked to select three dogs that he or she worked well with. The trainers looked for the emotional magic that creates a successful working partnership.

The staff do not look at the students' choices until they have discussed their own evaluations. First they rank each person according to the severity of his or her disability. Then they evaluate each dog and eliminate the ones that do not match the person's physical requirements, or do not bring out the student's emotional strengths. For example, Todd was matched with Cagney, because they felt the dog's independent, confident nature would bring out Todd's assertiveness. They were right: Controlling a large, strong-willed dog increased Todd's confidence in controlling his world. Barry, who lacked motivation, was forced to focus and concentrate his energy on Olympus, who was playful and lively.

When the trainers finish their evaluations, they open the student choices and complete the matching process. They keep all three of the student choices in reserve, in case they need to make additional changes.

How Dog Training Can Affect the Disabled

During the first training sessions, the students were asked to motivate the puppies without the use of leash corrections. (In ordinary dog obedience work, once the dog knows the task, it is reminded and corrected by a quick jerk of the leash.) In training independence companions, the staff wants the participants (many of whom may not have the ability to use leash corrections) to learn to use their voices and their feelings to attract and hold their dogs' attention. The staff also uses this training period to observe what the students will do when things get tough. Although the dogs have had months of previous training, the participants must learn how to get the dogs to obey *them*. This is frustrating, and often the students struggle to maintain their confidence. Even though the exercises are stressful, the fledgling trainers must not show this stress to the canines or the dogs will not obey.

"Focus yourself," Anthony said to the students when he could see their attention spans waning. "What do you want your dog to do? Get your dog's attention. Lighten your voice. Linda, if you say no to Dakota, she will say no to you. If your dog resists you, throw it off balance by changing the dynamic. Move in the other direction and encourage your dog to follow. Don't give up!"

While some students became discouraged, nobody gave up. Wheelchairs moved, voices strengthened, and slowly the dogs began to respond. The disabled students learned to take control of their dogs and to issue commands such as *get dressed* (the dog presents itself for the collar and backpack it carries each day); *go in* (the dog must lie quietly under a desk or table); *speak* (the dog must bark if there is an emergency); *go through* (the dog must move its body to pass through a door).

After a lunch break, the dogs were taken out on the grass. The students gave the dogs the command to eliminate: *Better go now*. Barry asked the instructor, "What if Olympus doesn't want to go now?" The trainer told Barry that he must learn how to read his dog's body language. It was a challenge for the boy, but one that he was sure to master. While the dogs learned to respond to the special needs of their partners, the students discovered their own emotional resources.

The staff then introduced the first use of leash correction. The students built on the morning work and used praise to get their dogs' attention. Finally, they used the leash to communicate what they wanted their dogs to do.

If the dog was hooked to a wheelchair, the owner was instructed to move the chair back and forth, tugging on the leash. If the dog was distracted, the student was told to turn and go in the other direction. In one instance, an instructor acted as a dog and attached himself to Barry's leash to give the youngster a feeling of how he could control his dog. In years of observing and participating in obedience training, I have never seen such an amazing training session. The students were determined to bond with their dogs and thus become independent.

After several days of training, the students were lectured on learning theories and then began to work on advanced commands. Each student threw a dumbbell so his or her dog could work on the fetch command: the dog must find the dumbbell, pick it up, hold it in its mouth, bring it back, and place it on the person's lap. The dogs made mistakes and the students got tired, but the trainers persisted with reminders to change tone of voice, avoid distraction, and so on.

The next training session took them outside to practice in a nearby shopping area among people and other distractions.

At the end of the two-week boot camp came "graduation." The nine graduating trainers sat on the platform in an auditorium filled with friends, family, and puppy raisers. The students had worked hard to earn their canine companions, and this was their celebration of that work. Each puppy raiser brought his or her dog to the platform and formally offered the leash to the graduate. It's not an easy moment for the foster family, but the experience of raising a puppy which will help out a disabled person is rewarding. The foster parent receives a certificate of appreciation. Many students stay in touch with their dog's original family and report on their progress. Both dogs and people have worked hard to develop a companion for independence.

BEST BREEDS FOR CANINE COMPANIONS

Experience in breeding and training has taught the CCI staff that some breeds are better suited to independence work than others. A strong willingness to work, however, is the main prerequisite for each dog that graduates.

These service dogs must pull wheelchairs, flip light switches, push elevator buttons, and retrieve dropped articles. The most commonly used breeds are Labrador and golden retrievers, because they are hardy and amiable, listen well, train easily, and can easily change their bonding from puppy raiser to trainer to handicapped owner. The CCI staff have also found that Doberman pinschers, Rottweilers, standard poodles, and German shepherds learn and work well. (Although shepherds are fast learners, they are not commonly used because they do not transfer their loyalty easily.)

Signal dogs must be aware of environmental sounds such as the telephone, a baby's cry, a knock on the door, an alarm clock, or a smoke alarm. CCI breeds the Pembroke Welsh corgi and the Border collie for this work, but they have found the schipperke, the Belgian sheepdog, and the Australian cattle dog to be good signal dogs as well. The corgi is especially successful because of its cocky, feisty independence. The Border collie works well because it can make sharp distinctions between different kinds of sounds.

Social dogs (which work in institutions and with convalescing, autistic, or developmentally disabled individuals) must provide companionship and help the owner relate to other people. These dogs need to enjoy cuddling and other contact with people. CCI has found that the black Labrador retriever is gregarious, outgoing, and eager to bond with the whole family. The standard poodle learns quickly and works well in convalescent hospitals, particularly for people with allergies. The golden retriever is friendly, easygoing, and eager to please.

While the CCI breeds specific dogs for specific tasks, the staff continues to experiment with other breeds. Temperament, good hips, and freedom from bone problems are particularly important in their breeding program.

BREEDING

When puppies are seven to eight weeks old, they are tested prior to entering foster homes. Puppies that score particularly well return to CCI at six months so the staff can determine if the puppy should take part in the breeding program. Those puppies not chosen for breeding continue their work training. Foster families that take part in the breeding program generally support the dog through three or four litters. Breeding dogs do not become working dogs; they remain with their foster families.

EVALUATING THE PUPPY

The dogs which will eventually become working dogs are tested at seven to eight weeks and retested when they are returned by their puppy raiser at sixteen to nineteen months.

The trainer tests the dogs to predict which ones will learn quickly and enjoy their work as canine companions. In addition, dogs are evaluated to see what type of companion work they would be best suited for. All dogs must be loving, intelligent, responsive, sensitive, and in good condition, but service dogs, for example, must also be submissive to their masters yet confident enough to work well with the public.

The exercises listed below were developed to assess the characteristics needed for service dog training.

1. *People Orientation*—The trainer places the puppy on the ground and encourages it to come. The trainer can ascertain if the dog is shy and if it chooses people over the environment.

2. *Willingness/Resistance to Being Handled*—The puppy is held by the trainer and its head is rotated. Since dogs carry their resistance in

their necks, the trainer notices if the puppy's neck stiffens and then measures the level of tension. The test also illustrates how much the puppy trusts people.

3. *Noise Sensitivity*—The trainer claps his hands over the dog's head and waits to see if the puppy will ignore the sound, become startled, or be curious enough to investigate. The test measures the puppy's ability to tolerate noise and still be curious.

4. *Ball Retrieval*—The trainer bounces a tennis ball and observes the puppy's reaction: Does the dog ignore it or retrieve it and bring it back to the trainer? The more dominant puppy will run away with it. A more submissive one (which is the type they look for) will bring it back.

5. *Problem Solving*—The puppy is placed in front of a barricade. A ball or a bit of food is thrown over it or someone calls the puppy from the other side. The trainer observes how quickly the puppy figures out that it must go around the barricade.

6. *Fear/Investigation*—This test utilizes a "Popcorn Popper" toy on wheels. The toy, which is odd-looking and makes a strange noise, is rolled on the ground in front of the puppy. The trainer watches to see if the puppy ignores the toy, investigates, or runs away. The ideal reaction is interest in the toy, with no sign of fearfulness. Data indicates that the results of this test predict if a puppy will be ideal breeding stock for the CCI program.

7. *Pain Tolerance/Forgiveness*—Pressure is put between the puppy's toes. The trainer observes how quickly the puppy "forgives" the tester for this act.

8. *Determination/Intelligence*—The puppy is held while someone throws a ball nearby. The trainer observes if the puppy will allow itself to be held back despite its interest in chasing the ball. The dog should be interested in the object but hold its curiosity in check. The ideal dog for the disabled owner will show interest in objects and yet be submissive to the commands of its owner.

9. *Dominance/Submission*—The puppy is held on its back for several minutes, allowing the trainer to show dominance. The puppy needs to be submissive enough to engage in training and interaction with its future disabled owner. CCI research indicates that breeding for this trait can show up within one generation of dogs.

10. *Sociability with Litter*—The trainer observes how friendly and playful the puppies are with their littermates. Fighting or shyness is not a desirable trait in CCI dogs.

Ruth Daniels, D.V.M., has researched the CCI tests and their ability to predict which dogs will graduate as assistance dogs and which will be suitable for future breeding stock (unpublished master's thesis, *Heritability of Behavior in Dogs with Reference to the Canine Companions for Independence Puppy Test*). Daniels found that dogs which graduated had significantly different test scores than those which were released from the program. Test #8 (Determination/Intelligence) was most valuable in tracing the inherited traits into the next generation and predicting which dogs would improve their skills.

Once the CCI dogs are trained and placed with their new owners, they can look forward to an average work career of about nine years. Retired dogs are kept by their masters or reunited with their puppy raisers. Producing a companion dog costs more than $7000; cost to the disabled owner is $125. The rest is paid by donations and grants.

Information on obtaining a dog or bringing up a puppy is available from Canine Companions for Independence, P.O. Box 446, Santa Rosa, California 95402-0446; telephone (707) 528-0830.

CHAPTER 13

Companion Dogs for Seniors

W HEN OLDER PEOPLE and dogs get together, there are often two benefits: the pet gains a home, the senior citizen a sense of comfort. For example, during the period of change after children move out of the home, a pet can help fill the void. Adjusting to a new lifestyle can be difficult, and the affectionate canine friend helps in this transitional period. Dogs can be talked to and can serve as the center of conversations with friends and family. A dog can help satisfy the elderly person's tactile needs as well. (Living alone and dealing with the loss of family members or close friends can cause an increase in the need for touching.) Dogs do not discriminate against the elderly; they are friendly to anyone who shows them affection. In addition, they provide a sense of safety and an incentive for regular exercise. Older people who live alone often skip meals; they are more likely to eat regularly when feeding a dog becomes a part of their daily schedule. Research shows that people like to talk to dog walkers, and this can pave the way for new friendships and activities outside the home.

An increasing number of studies show that caring for an animal can help maintain an older person's physical and mental health. Research shows that heart patients who own pets are more likely to be alive one year after a heart attack than those who don't. Studies also show that talking to or even just being next to a dog can significantly lower a person's blood pressure.

According to psychiatry professor Aaron Katcher, professor of animal ecology and director of the Center for Interaction of Animals and Society, animals can increase a person's resistance to disease (Katcher with Alan Beck, *Between Pets and People*, New York: Putnam, 1983). Dog ownership helps one avoid the "helplessness/hopelessness" syndrome associated with greater rates of invasive cancer and vulnerability to sudden death or accidents. Clearly, dogs and seniors need each other.

PETS FOR PEOPLE PROGRAM

One of the first programs that matched dogs to seniors was established in 1982 by the Missouri Humane Society in St. Louis and was called Golden Friendships. Potential pet owners over sixty years of age who qualified for the program did not have to pay the adoption fee, nor did they have to pay for the initial medical checkup, the necessary shots, or the mandatory spaying or neutering. The new dog owner received food and water dishes, a leash, and a starter supply of pet food. Free obedience classes were also available. Not every senior citizen could qualify for a pet under this program. The humane society wanted to know that the new pet owner would take good care of the dog. To that end, applicants were required to attend a short orientation class about the responsibilities of pet ownership, during which they learned about proper feeding, bathing, grooming, and exercise. Instructions for medical care and a procedure for care of the pet should they become unable to provide it were offered. Even after this orientation course, seniors did not automatically get to bring home a new dog. Participants were given time to think over the decision. Those who decided to acquire a dog were asked to specify the type of dog they wanted. When the right dog came into the shelter, the prospective owner returned and was introduced to the pet in a quiet room. If the match was successful, the dog went home.

A survey of two hundred of the program's first adopters showed that the pets did indeed seem to contribute to the health of the seniors. Almost 100 percent of the adopters said that their pets were good companions, 93 percent felt less lonely, 97 percent said they were happier, and 75 percent felt healthier.

Ralston-Purina, a St. Louis–based company which produces pet food, was impressed with the program (which was fast running out of financing) and took over the funding, renaming the program Pets for People. In addition, pilot programs were set up in other communities around the country. Since May 1987, Pets for People has operated through humane societies and public animal shelters in ninety cities, reimbursing each organization $100 for every animal adopted under its program.

PETS FOR PEOPLE'S ADOPTION PROCEDURE

All applicants to the program are carefully screened. The income level of the applicants does not determine eligibility. No particular breed of dog is recommended, only the size and disposition are suggested. The following guidelines are practiced:

1. Anyone over the age of sixty is eligible to adopt a pet.

2. Handicapped persons over sixty must pass the shelter's normal adoption screening procedures before joining the program.

3. The applicant must prove that he or she will personally (or with the aid of family or friend) be capable of providing the pet with safe and comfortable accommodations, a sound diet, adequate exercise, and transportation for periodic veterinary exams.

4. Those living in an apartment where space is limited should be willing to adopt pets that are tolerant of minimal living space.

5. The applicant must state the number of hours the pet will be alone each day and must present proof of landlord acceptance.

6. After the application has been completed, the senior attends one or two orientation sessions. (These sessions help reduce the return of pets.) After the session, a pet may be adopted immediately if a suitable one is available.

7. Within one week following adoption, the new owner is contacted and the matchup is evaluated. If there are any problems, the owner may come in with the pet to resolve them or switch the pet for a more appropriate one.

WHICH DOGS ARE BEST?

In nearly all cases, an adult dog is the appropriate pet for a senior. In the early months of the Friendship Program, almost all puppy adoptions were failures. Often the senior seeking a new dog had recently lost an older pet and had forgotten how lively and time-consuming a puppy could be. As a result, dogs need to be at least one year old. Dogs over one year are more likely to be housebroken and to have received some obedience training. People over sixty need dogs that can be easily managed on a leash and that will not trip them or knock them down.

For information on adopting a dog for a senior through the Pets for People program, call (800) 345-5678 or contact the Humane Society of Missouri, 1210 Macklind Avenue, St. Louis, MO 63110; telephone (314) 647-8800.

THE OLD FRIENDSHIPS PROGRAM

People over sixty-five years old and homeless dogs both have a guardian angel in the San Francisco SPCA. To help foster relationships between homeless adult pets and older people, the SF/SPCA offers an adoption service called the Old Friendships Program. It is available to anyone over sixty-five, regardless of income level or area of residence. Animals must be adopted from the SF/SPCA and be at least twelve months old at the time of adoption.

To encourage the success of its program, the SF/SPCA offers the following pet-related services and supplies to the qualified participants free of charge:

1. Adoption.

2. Basic veterinary care for one year at the SF/SPCA Hospital.

3. Initial supply of dog food.

4. Pet food coupons for life.

5. Spay/neuter surgery at the SF/SPCA Clinic.

6. First year's dog license.

7. Basic obedience classes provided by the San Francisco Dog Training Club.

8. Starter kit of supplies that includes bowls, collar, leash, and other miscellaneous supplies.

9. Grooming sessions for one year at the SF/SPCA Grooming College.

10. Behavioral consultation for life from the SF/SPCA Animal Behavior Hotline.

11. One-year membership to the SF/SPCA.

12. Pet Alert Card.

MEDICAL CARE PROGRAMS

The SF/SPCA offers a wide range of free medical care for the dogs in its seniors program. For people sixty-five and older who live on low fixed incomes, Pet-A-Care provides their pets with a comprehensive health care plan free of charge. Knowing that their dog will be well cared for is sometimes the turning point for a senior in choosing to own a companion dog. Along with the veterinary help, those dogs who are eligible for Pet-A-Care receive roundtrip transportation and free room and board for up to fourteen days at the SF/SPCA Hospital. For the elderly who don't drive or are in any way immobile, with no means of transportation, the SF/SPCA will transport their pets to their hospital at no charge.

PET FOOD PROGRAMS

The problem of getting to the grocery store to buy dog food may well deter a senior who would otherwise benefit from a dog companion. To help meet the needs of elderly, homebound pet owners, the SF/SPCA works with the Meals on Wheels program and the Home Health Project to provide free pet food and delivery for homebound or semi-ambulatory senior owners. There is a two-pet-per-household limit.

PET HOUSING ASSISTANCE

The San Francisco Housing Authority requires that pet owners who need housing pay a $100 pet deposit and that each dog be spayed or neutered, have annual veterinary checkups, and receive yearly vaccinations. For those seniors with limited incomes who might otherwise have to give up a dog under these circumstances, the SF/SPCA underwrites the cost of these requirements. If these elderly pet owners need dog care during a move or hospital stay, they can find free temporary housing for pets at the SF/SPCA for up to fourteen days.

The Old Friendships Program has found a way to make the adoption of a dog rewarding and successful for all participants. The lives of many older shelter dogs are saved, while the lives of the elderly are made richer with the companionship of an accepting friend.

Services offered in connection with this program are made possible solely through contributions to the SF/SPCA. For information on the Old Friendships Program, contact the San Francisco Society for the Prevention of Cruelty to Animals, 2500 Sixteenth Street, San Francisco, CA 94103; telephone (415) 554-3000.

OTHER ORGANIZATIONS

Another example of a successful community program that brings the elderly and animals together is PACT (People and Animals Coming Together). A volunteer from the Pennsylvania State University group interviews each person who requests a pet and then carefully matches an animal to that person's needs and abilities. Local veterinarians examine each animal, free of charge, before it is placed. Finally, the animal spends at least one week in the home of a PACT volunteer in order to make sure it has a good temperament and is properly trained. In addition, PACT provides a sponsor for each owner-pet pairing. This sponsor helps train the dog, takes it to the veterinarian, and may perform tasks such as bathing or grooming that older people might find difficult. The organization agrees to take the dog back if the owner becomes ill or if the two are not compatible.

Another group is the Pets are Wonderful Council (PAW), a nonprofit organization based in Chicago. This program is slightly different in that it matches young people with older adults who may need help caring for their pets. Paw Pals are youngsters who have completed a Boy Scout, Girl Scout, or 4-H pet care program and who know how to care for dogs. Paw Pals are matched to adults in their community, and walk, groom, or feed their dogs. Pet care sheets are provided so the children can keep careful records of their pet care duties. Besides providing pet care, this program is an ideal way to bridge the generation gap.

CANINE NURSING HOME THERAPISTS

Elderly persons who live in nursing homes, convalescent centers, or retirement homes benefit from canine "therapists." The pioneering work of psychologists Samuel Corson and Elizabeth O'Leary Corson showed that dogs in nursing homes provide love and tactile reassurance and that their childlike play is rejuvenating and reduces stress. They discovered that friendly and sociable dogs offered a more positive nonverbal message than even the most well-intentioned nursing home staff member. Not only did the dogs succeed in bringing depressed elderly patients out of their shells but they encouraged conversation between patients, diverting them from their worries and ills ("Companion Animals as Bonding Catalysts," by Corson and Corson, in *Geriatric Institutions in Interrelationships Between People and Pets*, eds. Bruce Fogle and Charles C. Thomas, Springfield, Il., 1981).

Veterinarian Leo K. Bustad, cofounder of the People-Pet-Partnership in Pullman, Washington, is president of the Delta Society and has pioneered pet therapy in geriatric and institutional settings. In the article that he coauthored with Linda M. Hines, "Placements of Animals with the Elderly: Benefits and Strategies," they describe how animals serve the needs of the elderly. They discuss how pets restore order to the lives of older people, linking their owners to a community of caring people and loving animals (*Guidelines: Animals in Nursing Homes*, Revised Edition, California Veterinary Medical Association, 1987).

Adopting a dog into a nursing home can help with the loneliness that the elderly often feel when they move from the familiarity of their homes to a strange new environment. Pets provide a multitude of recreational activities and opportunities for companionship. Feeding, walking, and talking to dogs dispel some of the loneliness and isolation that the elderly can experience in an institutionalized setting.

INTRODUCING A CANINE THERAPIST INTO A NURSING HOME

Placing a dog into a nursing home is not simple. Randall Lockwood, Ph.D., of the Humane Society of the United States, discusses in a Humane Society newsletter the need for guidelines and training for those involved with animals and the elderly ("Pet-Facilitated Therapy Grows Up," *The Humane Society News*, Spring 1986). The key to a successful program is good planning. Supervision and the welfare of the animals require ongoing evaluation, and volunteers offering pet services need proper training. Such planning is especially important when placing a dog as a full-time resident in a nursing home. Preparing staff members and residents for the responsibility of pet ownership is important.

Help in setting up a nursing home pet program is also available in a book edited by journalist Phil Arkow called *The Loving Bond: Companion Animals in the Helping Professions* (R&E Publishers, 1987). Another excellent resource is *Guidelines: Animals in Nursing Homes*, available from the Delta Society. It describes how to evaluate nursing homes using pet programs and details the steps necessary for effective placement and follow-up of the animals chosen.

PROGRAMS WHICH SPONSOR ANIMAL VISITS TO NURSING HOMES

In the past few years, human service agencies have become involved with pet therapy programs for the elderly. Baltimore's Pets on Wheels, for example, was organized in 1982 and is sponsored by the city's Commission on Aging and Retirement Education. This group uses carefully trained volunteers to visit area nursing homes with equally well-trained pets.

Some government organizations are turning to professional pet therapy groups to provide service to nursing homes. In 1984, the Pennsylvania Society for the Prevention of Cruelty to Animals and the Pennsylvania Women's SPCA turned their pet therapy programs over to Pals for Life, a nonprofit organization that specializes in bringing visiting animals to more than fifty nursing homes and senior citizen centers. Institutions that cannot afford to pay the group's minimal fee are supported by local businesses or by contributions from the United Way. Visiting dogs are owned by the Pals for Life staff, and those animals that become nursing home residents are supervised and trained by the group's staff members.

There are many other programs across the country which successfully involve the community in bringing animals and nursing home residents together. For example, PALS, located in Boise, Idaho, has an educational program in which young people visit nursing home residents with their animals. Students from the Scouts organizations, 4-H club, and the YMCA also have the option of attending training sessions that teach them how to deal with the physical limitations of the elderly. Companion Animal Partnership, a program at Washington State University, sponsors students and other volunteers who take pets chosen largely from a pet-lending roster to nursing homes for visits. This program also offers dog shows and obedience demonstrations on the grounds of the nursing homes. Therapy Dogs International, in Hillside, New Jersey, registers dogs whose owners take them to visit the elderly and the emotionally disabled. Membership is open to dog owners as well as animal lovers in the community.

As the need for and the use of canine therapists for the elderly increases, research and community involvement will continue to grow. Guidelines and suggestions for people who wish to start such a program or organization are available from the Delta Society, P. O. Box 1080, Renton, WA 98057; telephone (206) 226-7357. Another excellent source is the Latham Foundation, Latham Plaza Building, Clement and Schiller, Alameda, CA 94501; telephone (415) 521-0920.

SELECTING A COMPANION FOR A SENIOR CITIZEN

The right dog for an older person can provide companionship and a sense of well-being. It is clear from the experiences of the organizations described above that careful selection and planning for the dog's welfare are important. In fact, not every senior citizen needs a dog. In some cases, a small animal such as a cat or a bird or fish is the more appropriate pet. Neither the dog nor the senior is helped by an adoption that fails.

The following guidelines can help match the dog to the needs of the senior citizen.

1. The ideal dog for an elderly person is well socialized, easygoing, calm, and friendly. This is a dog that will give pleasure and companionship, not problems, to the new owner.

2. Choose a dog over one year of age that is fairly well housetrained. Arrange for further obedience work through the Humane Society or local obedience club. Both are excellent sources of information and support for the senior's ongoing relationship with the new dog.

3. Match the size of the dog to the senior's ability to control and exercise it. A lively dog that could knock down an older person or pull the owner into the street is not appropriate. Daily walks will be good for both the dog and the owner, so the elderly person needs to have a canine that is well under control in the outdoors.

4. A feeding schedule needs to be set up, stating the appropriate amount of food. Some seniors tend to overindulge their pets, which results in canine obesity or poor health. This can be prevented by established guidelines for the dog's diet.

5. Check the dog's grooming needs. Know in advance how the dog will be bathed and brushed. If the dog requires professional grooming, make a plan for budgeting this item and for transportation to and from the groomer.

6. Choose a veterinarian who is responsive to the needs of both the dog and the senior. An understanding veterinarian can be helpful in let-

ting the owner maintain a dog's good health. Make arrangements for transportation to and from the veterinarian.

7. If the senior has ongoing health problems, set up a plan for the care of the dog in case of the owner's illness or hospitalization. This prevents the owner from excessive worry and provides adequate care for the dog.

8. After the dog is adopted, it is helpful for the senior to have ongoing contact with the adoption agency. This open communication line can help with any adjustment problems and help the adoption continue to be successful.

14

Dog Actors

Today, there is an increasing demand for canines with good looks and personality to costar in commercials and movies. The tradition of performing dogs dates back to the seventeenth century, when dogs, as "tumblers," accompanied dancers and acrobats in shows. Intelligent poodles did tricks, walked on their hind legs in costumes, and even learned to dance to music. Punch and Judy puppet shows during the 1800s featured a dog named Toby who protected his master Punch and would not only shake hands but also sing an occasional tune.

One of the best known Hollywood canine stars was Rin Tin Tin. Before his acting career, this versatile German shepherd served the military as a messenger in World War I. His career in films spanned fourteen years, during which he was so famous that he signed his contracts with his own paw print! When he died in 1932, his fans heard a news release which began: "The most celebrated dog in the world has left to go to the hunting grounds in the Elysian fields."

Just before World War II, another dog star made "her" debut, a long-haired collie named Lassie (actually, the dog was male). This canine starred in a number of children's movies and a long-running television show, and in fact, his contract guaranteed that he work no more than seven hours a day! His look was so popular that casting directors to this day often request a "Lassie" type when canine roles are up for grabs.

Hollywood dogs are not members of the Screen Actors Guild (SAG), but their trainers must belong to Teamsters Union #399. If a dog is needed in a movie, the production department or property master calls a trainer and asks for a dog that meets the script's specifications, for instance, a sheepdog that speaks, a mutt, or a collie like Lassie.

According to animal trainer Kim Lindemoen, different looks in dogs are popular from year to year. One of her dogs is Winston, a male English bull terrier (a Spuds MacKenzie look-alike) who can roll over, play dead, sit up, speak, and shake hands. Another is Champion Kodiak, a brown Newfoundland who has professional screen credits (*Police Academy II*). With five obedience titles, he started his career at age four. Within two weeks, he had learned to pull on a pant leg, alert, simulate an attack, and speak with a "serious bark."

To begin an acting career, dogs first need obedience training. Once they complete their basic training, they are enrolled in a ten-week "acting" class called "trick training." In this class, they learn to "speak," put their heads down, jump through hoops, back out, remember and go to a "point," and carry objects. They must practice with a number of people because they need to learn how to perform and be sociable with anyone. No one fails at this course, but some dogs are better at some tricks than others. For instance, a large dog may not be able to sit up, but he can learn to speak with authority.

The dogs are then listed in a directory and available to be called. Unfortunately, only 25 percent of the graduates make it to the screen. But those not called for film or TV roles can still find work. Some perform at children's birthday parties, others perform for the handicapped and at convalescent homes.

Generally, movie and TV audiences like to see "all-American" dogs, so mixed breeds tend to get the most work. The German shepherd and the collie are the most popular purebred types because of their screen star history. The golden retriever is also a popular breed (for its outdoor look). Few dogs make it big, but a star like Mike (*Down And Out in Beverly Hills*) can earn anywhere from $1500 to $2500 per week.

Although the dogs don't belong to a guild, they always have a representative on the movie set to protect their welfare. In 1979, the American Humane Association convinced the board of the Screen Actors Guild that animal cruelty was still being practiced. As a result, an animal clause, which was also approved by the producers, is now included in every SAG contract. It states that "the producer shall notify the American Humane Association prior to the commencement of any work involving an animal and advise it of the nature of the work to be performed. Script scenes involving animals shall be made available to the American Humane Association and a representative may be present at any time during the filming of a motion picture with animals."

CHOOSING AN ACTING PUPPY

If you want to acquire a puppy actor, below are some guidelines that you can follow that have been successful for owners with such canines.

1. Choose the most outgoing puppy in the litter. Don't pick the aggressive one but look for one which wants to play. If one puppy is lively and the rest are asleep, the alert one may be ready for the camera.

2. Look for the dog that communicates, "pick me up." Animal actors need to know how to communicate.

3. Test the puppy for sound sensitivity. Clap over its head and see if it reacts with fear. (There are always lights and noises on the set that the puppy will need to accept.)

4. Test the puppy's curiosity. Bring a large interesting toy and put it on the ground; watch to see if the puppy investigates. It is easier to train a puppy with a high degree of curiosity.

5. Bring a ball for a quick game of retrieval. Puppies that enjoy retrieving are good trick training candidates.

6. Bring a treat. Since the puppy will be trained with food treats, you need a puppy that likes food. Finicky eaters do not train well.

Puppy training for performing dogs starts at eight weeks. By four months, the puppy should be able to respond to such commands as *sit up*, *speak*, *put head down*, *jump up*, *look interested*, and *stay*. All tasks are learned by food reward. (The best treats are hot dogs and fried liver. Cookies work for some dogs, but an acting candidate gets bored with ordinary cookies. Trainers often put a little garlic salt on the cookie to give it a gourmet appeal.)

EVALUATING AN ADULT DOG FOR ACTING

Look for temperament. The dog actor needs to be friendly and outgoing. Because of the number of people it will work with, it must have a flexible personality.

Looks are also important. Keep the following in mind:

1. Shaggy dogs are popular, so if you have a purebred that is usually clipped for the conformation ring, don't clip it for the movies.

2. If the ears stand up, they may give the canine personality an interesting expression. Even one ear up and one down attracts attention.

3. There are a few calls for big dogs like St. Bernards, but most requests are for small to medium-sized dogs.

4. Purebreds with long hair can respond to different requests depending on their haircuts. Often purebreds are more popular if they have a "mutt" look.

If your dog takes a trick class and doesn't make it to the screen, don't be discouraged. Entertaining at home can make your dog the life of any party. Visiting the elderly and convalescent homes offers its own rewards while continuing the tradition of the theater.